EYEWITNESS *Travel Guides*

MANDARIN
CHINESE
PHRASE BOOK

A DK Publishing Book
www.dk.com

A DK PUBLISHING BOOK

www.dk.com

Compiled by Lexus Ltd with Huiqun Ye and Lesley Thirkell

First American Edition, 1999
2 4 6 8 10 9 7 5 3 1

Published in the United States by DK Publishing, Inc.
95 Madison Avenue, New York, New York 10016

Copyright © 1999 Dorling Kindersley Limited, London

Library of Congress Cataloging-in-Publication Data
Mandarin Chinese phrase book / [compiled] by Lexus Ltd. with
Huiqun Ye and Lesley Thirkell.
    p.   cm. -- (Eyewitness travel guides)
    ISBN 0–7894–4188–8 (alk. paper)
    1. Chinese language--Conversation and phrase books--English.
    2. China--Guidebooks. I. Ye, Huiqun.   II. Thirkell, Lesley.
    III. Lexus (firm) IV. Series.
PL1125.E6M28 1999
495.1'83421--dc21   98–53896
                                                              CIP

Picture Credits
Jacket: all images special photography Paul Williams except
BRITSTOCK IFA: Eric Bach front center left; Bernd Ducke front bottom
right and back left; IMPACT: Christophe Bluntzer front center left above;
Michael Good front top/center right; Mark Henley front center/
bottom left; Alain Le Gasmeur spine, back right.

Printed and bound in Italy by Printer Trento Srl.

CONTENTS

PREFACE

This *Eyewitness Travel Guide Phrase Book* has been compiled by experts to meet the general needs of tourists and business travelers. Arranged under headings such as Hotels, Driving, and so forth, the Mandarin Chinese words and phrases are printed in Pinyin, the standard system of romanization. Chinese characters are also shown, except in the *Things You'll Hear* boxes. Although plenty of guidance is given regarding pronunciation (see pages 5–6), there are some tricky tones to master. There are other Chinese dialects in addition to Mandarin, such as Cantonese. These use the same characters, but the pronunciation is very different, so making yourself understood in some regions might be difficult. If you feel unsure of yourself, simply point to the phrase you want to say.

Of course, you will want to know what signs and notices mean when they are written in Chinese characters. There are lists of common signs (pages 14–15) and road signs (page 30) as well as recognition boxes headed *Things You'll See* in most sections of the book. These cover words, signs, notices, etc.; the Chinese script is given alongside its Pinyin version and the English translation.

A 1,200-line mini-dictionary will help you form additional phrases (or help you express the one word you need), and the extensive Menu Guide will ease your way through complicated Chinese meals, which can be a world apart from those you find in your local takeout. Under the heading Cross-Cultural Notes you will find guidance on aspects of the Chinese way of life. An understanding of such matters will enhance your trip to China, and your hosts will appreciate all the effort you have made to respect their culture and to speak their language.

Eyewitness Travel Guides are recognized as the world's best travel guides. Each title features specially commissioned color photographs, cutaways of major buildings, 3-D aerial views, and detailed maps, plus information on sights, events, hotels, restaurants, shopping, and entertainment.

PRONUNCIATION

In this phrase book, Pinyin spelling is used. Pinyin is the usual method for writing Mandarin in the Roman alphabet, but it is not a pronunciation system. The following consists of guidelines for pronouncing Pinyin:

CONSONANTS

c	like "ts" in "sets"
q	like "ch" in "China"
x	like "sh" in "shoe"
z	like "ds" in "beds"
zh	like "j" in "Jane"

VOWELS AND VOWEL COMBINATIONS

a	as in "father"
ai	as in "Shanghai"
ei	as in "Beijing" or "eight"
i	as in "Maria" except in the following combinations: ci, chi, ri, si, shi, zi, and zhi when it is pronounced as in "sir"
ia	as "ya" in "yard"
ian	pronounced "yen"
iang	pronounced "yahng"
ie	pronounced as Old English "yea"
iu	as "yo" in "yoke"
o	as in "for"
ou	as in "though"
u	as in "too" (but in some instances as in ü below)
ui	pronounced "way"
uo	pronounced "war"
ü	as in "few" (also as in the German word "über" or the French word "du")

TONES

Mandarin is a tonal language and has four tones. That means sounds can be pronounced with four different types of intonation. The first tone is flat and continuous, as if briefly holding the same musical note. The second is a rising tone similar to the intonation of a question, for example, "why?" The third tone falls, then rises, resembling a note of surprise as in "What!" The fourth is a falling tone like the tone of an emphatic "No!" in English.

First ‾ Second ´ Third ˇ Fourth `

Each Mandarin word has its own written character and a fixed tone in the spoken language. Mistakes can lead to a degree of confusion in spoken (although not in written) Mandarin since tones can affect meaning:

> mǎi is "to buy" and mài is "to sell"
> mǎ is "horse" and mā is "mother"
> táng is "sugar" and tāng "soup"

CROSS-CULTURAL NOTES

MEETING CHINESE PEOPLE

Visitors to China are usually surprised by the considerable attention paid to foreigners. Although this can be very intimidating, it is just curiosity, particularly if the foreigner has blond hair, a beard, or is tall. Trying to communicate with the "audience," or even trying to take their photo, can help disperse the crowd.

The Mandarin equivalents of "Mr." and "Mrs." are rarely used, so it can be quite hard to know how to address people, particularly in a formal situation. Generally, a person's surname is followed by their job title. So Mr. Li Hong (surname first), a teacher, would be called Li Lǎoshī. Among friends, people are often called young (xiǎo) or old (lǎo), depending on their relationship to the speaker. So, a younger friend might be called Xiǎo Li, and an older or more respected person, Lǎo Li. If in doubt, use the whole name.

Chinese people are very hospitable and sometimes invite foreigners to visit, eat in, or stay in their homes. If invited, it is polite to accept, but be aware that while it is now technically legal for foreigners to stay in Chinese people's homes without specific police permission, you could cause your host a great deal of trouble with the authorities.

The Chinese find expensive gifts embarrassing, but it would be acceptable to offer such things as foreign postage stamps or cassettes of Western music.

CONVERSATION

Most young people have studied English, although it is sometimes easier to communicate by writing things down because students rarely learn to speak or listen to English at school. Many people seize every opportunity to practice their English on a native speaker. This can become irritating, but can also help you meet some interesting people. When chatting with Chinese people, topics such as family, marital status, income, life at home, and opinions of China are popular. Do not insist on discussing politics, particularly in public places, unless all the people you are with seem happy to do so.

DRESS

Scanty clothing is generally frowned upon, particularly in the countryside, when worn by either foreigners or young Chinese.

PERSONAL CONDUCT AND MANNERS

Overt displays of affection, such as kissing in a public, can be regarded as offensive. Chinese table manners are fairly lax, but gesticulating with chopsticks should be avoided.

RESTROOMS

Although tourist hotels provide Western-style restrooms, most other restrooms tend to have fairly primitive squat toilets. Many Chinese homes do not have a private bathroom, so public restrooms are very common and easy to find. It is advisable to carry a supply of toilet paper with you at all times.

PHOTOGRAPHS

Military and strategic sites (for example, bridges, harbors, etc.) must not be photographed. Otherwise, photographs can be taken freely, but you should be tactful, since many old people find being photographed very distressing.

TRAVEL

It is necessary to be patient and easygoing while traveling in China, since conditions can be very stressful. It is important to realize that more can be achieved by being calm and friendly, especially when buying tickets, which can be a very time-consuming business. Occasionally, Chinese people will offer to help with your problem.

RESTRICTED AREAS

Certain areas of China are closed to foreigners. Going to these areas without a travel permit from the police can result in deportation. The number of "open" areas has increased dramatically over the years and now most areas of interest to foreign tourists are open. Generally, areas are closed because of poverty, or a lack of facilities deemed suitable for foreigners, or for military reasons.

RELIGION

Officially there is religious freedom in China. There are large numbers of Muslims, and Xinjiang and Ningxia are Autonomous Islamic Regions. Similarly, Tibet and its surrounding areas are strongly Tibetan Buddhist. Monks usually welcome foreigners who wish to visit temples. Throughout China there are also small pockets of Christians, both Catholic and Protestant. However, in most of China, religion is not an important facet of life.

USEFUL EVERYDAY PHRASES

Yes/no

In Mandarin there is no single word for "yes" or "no." Instead, the verb from the question is repeated as the affirmative. For "no," the negative word "*bù*" is used before the verb from the question. For example: "do you want . . .?" (*nǐ yào bú yào . . .?*)— "yes" = "*yào*," "no" = "*bú yào*," "are you . . .?" (*nǐ shì bú shì*)— "yes" = "*shì*," "no" = "*bú shì*." The only exception is with the verb "to have." Instead of "*bù*," use the word "*méi*." For example: "do you have . . .?" (*ní yǒu méi yǒu?*)—"yes" = "*yǒu*"; "no" = "*méi yǒu*."

Thank you
Xièxie
谢谢

No, thank you
Bù, xièxie
不要, 谢谢

Please
Qǐng
请

Please (*accepting*)
Yào
要

I don't understand
Wǒ bù dǒng
我不懂

Do you speak English?
Nǐ shuō yīngyǔ ma?
你说英语吗?

I can't speak Chinese
Wǒ búhuì shuō Hànyǔ
我不会说汉语

I don't know
Wǒ bù zhīdào
我不知道

Please speak more slowly
Qǐng shuō màn yí diǎn
请说慢一点

Please write it down for me
Qíng nǐ géi wó xiěyíxià
请你给我写一下

My name is . . .
Wǒ jiào . . .
我叫...

How do you do, pleased to meet you
Ní hǎo, hěn gāoxìng rènshí nǐ
你好，很高兴认识你

Good morning/good afternoon/good evening
Ní hǎo
你好

Good night
Wǎn ān
晚安

Good-bye
Zàijiàn
再见

11

How are you?
Ní hǎo ma?
你好吗?

Excuse me, please *(to get attention)*
Láojià
劳驾

Sorry!
Duìbùqǐ
对不起!

I'm really sorry
Zhēn duìbùqǐ
真对不起

Can you help me?
Nǐ néng bù néng bāngzhù wǒ?
你能不能帮助我?

Can you tell me . . .?
Nǐ néng bù néng gàosù wǒ . . .?
你能不能告诉我...?

Can I have . . .?
Wǒ néng bù néng yào . . .?
我能不能要...?

I would like . . .
Wó xiǎng yào . . .
我想要...

Is there . . . here?
Zhèlǐ yǒu méi yǒu . . .?
这里有没有...?

Where can I get . . .?
Nálǐ yǒu . . .?
哪里有...?

How much is it?
Duōshǎo qián?
多少钱?

What time is it?
Xiànzài jí diǎn zhōng?
现在几点钟?

I must go now
Wǒ déi zǒu le
我得走了

I'm lost
Wǒ mí lù le
我迷路了

Cheers! *(toast)*
Gānbēi!
干杯!

Do you take credit cards?
Kéyǐ yòng xìnyòngkǎ ma?
可以用信用卡吗?

Where is the restroom?
Cèsuǒ zài nálǐ?
厕所在哪里?

Go away!
Zǒu kāi!
走开!

Excellent!
Hǎo jí le!
好极了!

THINGS YOU'LL HEAR

Méiyǒu	We don't have any
Bùxíng	It's not possible
Dāngxīn	Look out!
Bú kèqì	You're welcome
Huānyíng	Welcome
Xièxie	Thanks
Duìbuqǐ	Excuse me
Ní hǎo, hěn gāoxìng rènshi nǐ	How do you do, nice to meet you
Zàijiàn	Good-bye
Méi guānxì	It doesn't matter
Láojià	Excuse me
Wǒ bù dǒng	I don't understand
Wǒ bù zhīdào	I don't know
Zěnme le?	What's the matter?
Yào bú yào?	Do you want it?

THINGS YOU'LL SEE

办公室	bàngōngshì	office
不营业	bù yíngyè	not open for business
厕所	cèsuǒ	restroom
出口	chūkǒu	exit
电梯	diàntī	elevator
付款台	fùkuǎn tái	pay here

→

坏了	huàile	out of order
静	jìng	silence (in hospitals, libraries)
禁止拍照	jìnzhǐ pāizhào	no photographs!
军事要地, 　请勿靠近	jūnshì yàodì, qǐng wù kàojìn!	military zone, keep out!
开	kāi	open
开放时间	kāifàng shíjiān	opening times
拉	lā	pull
男	ná	men's restroom
女	nǚ	women's restroom
票	piào	tickets
入口	rùkǒu	way in
上	shàng	up
收款台	shōu kuǎn tái	cash register (check out)
太平门	tàipíngmén	emergency exit
推	tuī	push
外宾止步	wàibīn zhǐbù	no foreigners allowed
危险	wēixiǎn!	danger!
下	xià	down
营业时间	yíngyè shíjiān	business hours
游人止步	yóurén zhǐbù	private

DAYS, MONTHS, SEASONS

Sunday	xīngqītiān	星期天
Monday	xīngqīyī	星期一
Tuesday	xīngqīèr	星期二
Wednesday	xīngqīsān	星期三
Thursday	xīngqīsì	星期四
Friday	xīngqīwǔ	星期五
Saturday	xīngqīliù	星期六

January	yīyuè	一月
February	èryuè	二月
March	sānyuè	三月
April	sìyuè	四月
May	wǔyuè	五月
June	liùyuè	六月
July	qīyuè	七月
August	bāyuè	八月
September	jiǔyuè	九月
October	shíyuè	十月
November	shíyīyuè	十一月
December	shíèryuè	十二月

Spring	chūntiān	春天
Summer	xiàtiān	夏天
Fall	qiūtiān	秋天
Winter	dōngtiān	冬天

Christmas	shèngdàn jié	圣诞节
New Year	yuándàn	元旦
Chinese New Year	chūn jié	春节
National Day	guóqìng jié	国庆节
The Mid-Autumn Festival	zhōngqiū jié	中秋节
Chinese New Year's Eve	dànián sānshí	大年三十

NUMBERS

0	líng	零		10	shí	十
1	yī	一		11	shíyī	十一
2	èr/liǎng	二 / 两		12	shíèr	十二
3	sān	三		13	shísān	十三
4	sì	四		14	shísì	十四
5	wǔ	五		15	shíwǔ	十五
6	liù	六		16	shíliù	十六
7	qī	七		17	shíqī	十七
8	bā	八		18	shíbā	十八
9	jiǔ	九		19	shíjiǔ	十九

20	èrshí	二十
21	èrshíyī	二十一
22	èrshíèr	二十二
30	sānshí	三十
31	sānshíyī	三十一
32	sānshíèr	三十二
40	sìshí	四十
50	wǔshí	五十
60	liùshí	六十
70	qīshí	七十

80	bāshí	八十	110	yìbǎi yìshí	一百一十
90	jiǔshí	九十	111	yìbǎi shíyī	一百十一
100	yìbǎi	一百	120	yìbǎi èrshí	一百二十
101	yìbǎi líng yī	一百零一	200	èrbǎi	二百
			300	sānbǎi	三百

1000	yìqiān	一千
10,000	yíwàn	一万
20,000	èrwàn	二万
100,000	shíwàn	十万
1,000,000	yī bǎiwàn	一百万
10,000,000	qiānwàn	一千万
100,000,000	yí yì	一亿

Note that Mandarin has a unit for 10,000, a "*wàn*," for example: 10,000 is "*yí wàn*" (literally one x 10,000) and 100,000 is "*shí wàn*" (literally 10 x 10,000). Note also that there are two words for "2." In a counting sequence (1-2-3-4) use "*èr*." But when referring to two objects, two people, etc use "*liǎng*," So, for example, "I want two tickets" is "*wǒ yào liǎng zhāng piào*."

MEASURE WORDS

Mandarin uses counting, or measure, words between the number and the noun. For example, "one ticket" is "*yì zhāng piào*" where "*zhāng*" is the measure word for "ticket"; "two horses" is "*liǎng pí mǎ*" where "*pí*" is the measure word for "horses." There are a great number of measure words, the use of which depends on the type of object being talked about. A general measure word is "*gè*" which, while not always technically correct, can be used in most contexts.

TIME

today	jīntiān	今天
yesterday	zuótiān	昨天
tomorrow	míngtiān	明天
the day before yesterday	qiántiān	前天
the day after tomorrow	hòutiān	后天
this week	zhège xīngqī	这个星期
last week	shàngge xīngqī	上个星期
next week	xiàge xīngqī	下个星期
this morning	jīntiān shàngwǔ	今天上午
this afternoon	jīntiān xiàwǔ	今天下午
this evening	jīntiān wǎnshàng	今天晚上
tonight	jīnwǎn	今晚
yesterday afternoon	zuótiān xiàwǔ	昨天下午
last night	zuótiān wǎnshàng	昨天晚上
fortnight	liǎngge xīngqī	两个星期
six months	bànnián/liùgeyuè	半年／六个月
tomorrow morning	míngtiān shàngwǔ	明天上午
tomorrow night	míngtiān wǎnshàng	明天晚上
in three days	sāntiān hòu	三天后
three days ago	sāntiān qián	三天前
late	wǎn/chí	晚／迟

early	zǎo	早
soon	kuài	快
later on	yǐhòu	以后
at the moment	xiànzài	现在
second	miǎo	秒
minute	fēn	分
one minute	yì fēnzhōng	一分钟
two minutes	liǎng fēnzhōng	两分钟
quarter of an hour	yí kèzhōng	一刻钟
half an hour	bàn xiǎoshí	半小时
three quarters of an hour	sān kèzhōng	三刻钟
hour	xiǎoshí	小时
that day	nà tiān	那天
every day	měitiān	每天
all day	zhěngtiān	整天
the next day	dì'èrtiān	第二天

TELLING TIME

In Mandarin, "*diăn zhōng*" corresponds to the word "o'clock" and follows the number. To show time after the hour, simply add the number of minutes, without "*zhōng*": "three twenty" is "*sān diăn èr shí.*"

However, up to ten past the hour, the word for "minute," "*fēn,*" should also be added. So, for example, "ten past three" is "*sān diăn shí fēn.*" "Past" is "*guò,*" "quarter" is "*yíkè,*" so "quarter past three" is "*sāndiăngùo yíkè.*" "To" is "*chà,*" so quarter to three is "*sāndiăn chà yíkè.*" Half is "*bàn*" so "half past three" is "*sān diăn bàn.*"

Timetables and other official lists use the twenty-four hour clock, written in Arabic numerals (as used in Europe).

Note that for "two" the word "*liăng*" is used in telling time, not "*èr.*"

AM	shàngwŭ
PM	xiàwŭ
one o'clock	yī diănzhōng
ten past one	yīdiăn shífēn
quarter past one	yīdiăn guò yíkè
half past one	yīdiăn bàn
twenty to two	liángdiăn chà èrshífēn
quarter to two	liángdiăn chà yíkè
two o'clock	liángdiănzhōng
13:00	xiàwŭ yīdiăn zhōng
16:30	xiàwŭ sìdiăn bàn
at half past five	wŭdiăn bàn
at seven o'clock	qī diănzhōng
noon	zhōngwŭ
midnight	bànyè

For dates add "*hào*" to the number, for example:

11th	shíyīhào

HOTELS

In China, there are many different types of hotel, ranging from international joint venture hotels to very basic youth hostel-like accommodations. International standard luxury hotels, often known as "*bīnguǎn*," charge international rates and are almost exclusively for foreign visitors. There are also many high-quality nationally owned hotels, often called "*fàndiàn*," which provide a good or high degree of comfort and service. These hotels admit both foreign and Chinese guests. The more basic hotels, usually called "*lǚguǎn*," offer very inexpensive accommodations, but often these will not allow foreigners to stay without a great deal of persuasion. Only certain hotels have permission to admit foreigners, and in many areas this law is strictly enforced.

Chinese hotels rarely provide rooms with a double bed, so you would have to make a point of asking for this. Expect to find rooms with twin beds or, in the lower-grade hotels, rooms with four, six and eight beds or even dormitories. Meals are rarely included in the price of a room, although most hotels have a restaurant, serving at specific times only. Bathroom and shower facilities are rarely private, and you will usually find that they are situated along the corridor.

USEFUL WORDS AND PHRASES

balcony	yángtái	阳台
bathroom	yùshì	浴室
bed	chuáng	床
bedroom	wòshì	卧室
bill	zhàngdān	帐单
breakfast	zǎofàn	早饭
dining room	cāntīng	餐厅
dinner	wǎncān	晚餐

dormitory	tǒng pù fángjiān	统铺房间
dormitory bed	tǒng pù	统铺
double bed	shuāngrén chuáng	双人床
double room	shuāngrén fángjiān	双人房间
elevator	diàntī	电梯
hotel	fàndiàn	饭店
key	yàoshi	钥匙
lobby	xiūxītīng	休息厅
lounge	xiūxīshì	休息室
lunch	wǔfàn	午饭
manager	jīnglǐ	经理
reception	jiēdàitái	接待台
receptionist	jiēdàiyuán	接待员
restaurant	cānguǎn	餐馆
room	fángjiān	房间
room service	sòng fàn fúwù	送饭服务
shower	línyù	淋浴
single room	dānrén fángjiān	单人房间
toilet/restroom	cèsuǒ	厕所
twin room	yǒu liǎngzhāng chuáng dai fángjiān	有两张床的房间

Do you have any vacancies?
Hái yǒu kōng fángjiān ma?
还有空房间吗?

I have a reservation
Wó yǐjīng yùdìngle fángjiān
我已经预订了房间

I'd like a single/twin room
Wó xiăngyào yíge dānrén/yŏu liăngzhāng chuáng dai fángjiān
我想要一个单人 / 有两张床的房间

I'd like a room with a double bed
Wó xiăngyào yíge yŏu shuāngrén chuáng de fángjiān
我想要一个有双人床的房间

I'd like a bed in the dormitory
Wó xiăngyào yíge tŏng pù
我想要一个统铺

I'd like a room with a bathroom/balcony
Wó xiăngyào yígè dài yùshì/yángtái de fángjiān
我想要一个带浴室 / 阳台的房间

I'd like a room for one night/three nights
Wó xiăngyào yígè fángjiān zhù yíyè/sānyè
我想要一个房间住一夜 / 三夜

What is the charge per night?
Duōshăo qián yíyè?
多少钱一夜？

I don't know yet how long I'll stay
Wŏ hái bù zhīdào wŏ yào dāi duōjiŭ
我还不知道我要呆多久

When is breakfast/dinner?
Jídiăn chī zăofàn/wănfàn?
几点吃早饭 / 晚饭？

Would you have my baggage brought up?
Qĭng sòng yíxià xínglĭ, hăoma?
请送一下行李, 好吗？

Please call me at . . . o'clock
Qǐng zài . . . diǎn jiào wǒ yíxià
请在...点叫我一下

May I have breakfast in my room?
Wǒ kéyǐ zài zìjǐ fángjiānlǐ yòng zǎocān ma?
我可以在自己房间里用早餐吗？

I'll be back at . . . o'clock
Wǒ . . . diǎn huílái
我...点回来

My room number is . . .
Wǒde fángjiān hàomǎ shì . . .
我的房间号码是...

I'm leaving tomorrow
Wǒ míngtiān líkāi zhèr
我明天离开这儿

May I have the bill, please?
Qǐng géi wǒ jiéyíxià zhàng, hǎoma?
请给我结一下帐，好吗？

I'll pay by credit card
Wó xiǎng yòng xìnyòngkǎ fùzhàng
我想用信用卡付帐

Can you get me a taxi?
Nǐ néng bāng wǒ jiào liàng chūzūchē ma?
你能帮我叫辆出租车吗？

Can you recommend another hotel?
Nǐ néng géi wǒ tuījiàn qítā fàndiàn ma?
你能给我推荐其它饭店吗？

THINGS YOU'LL SEE

安全门	ānquánmén	emergency exit
餐馆	cānguǎn	restaurant
厕所	cèsuǒ	toilet, restroom
电梯	diàntī	elevator
接待台	jiēdàitái	reception
客满	kèmǎn	no vacancies
拉	lā	pull
淋浴	línyù	shower
盆浴	pényù	bath
推	tuī	push
洗手间	xíshǒujiān	washroom
一层	yīcéng	ground floor

THINGS YOU'LL HEAR

Duìbuqǐ, kèmǎnle
I'm sorry, we're full

Méiyǒu dānrén fángjiānle
There are no single rooms left

Zhù jǐyè?
For how many nights?

Qǐng yùxiān fùkuǎn
Please pay in advance

DRIVING

Foreigners are allowed to rent cars for local use in some major cities, but considerable restrictions will apply. You will need an international driver's license, and may only drive within designated boundaries. The easiest and most common way to travel by car is to rent one complete with driver. Many hotels have taxis for this purpose.

Traffic rules, particularly outside large cities, tend to be very lax. Drive on the right, pass on the left. At traffic lights, traffic turning right should drive on—there is no need to stop for the lights. Traffic coming onto a traffic circle has priority.

Speed limits vary from area to area, and are rarely adhered to. In towns, the limit is generally as low as 30km/h (19 mph). Out of towns, the limit is approximately 60km/h (37 mph). It is against the law to drive without a seat belt.

China has few Western-style gas stations. Usually gas is bought from government-controlled outlets and it can be very difficult for an individual to purchase gas, so before renting any kind of vehicle, it is vital to make sure you have enough fuel for your trip.

USEFUL WORDS AND PHRASES

breakdown	gùzhàng	故障
car	xiǎoqìchē	小汽车
to drive	kāichē	开车
garage (*for repairs*)	qìchē xiūlíchǎng	汽车修理厂
gas	qìyóu	汽油
gas station	jiāyóuzhàn	加油站
license	jiàshǐ zhízhào	驾驶执照
van	péngchē	篷车

I'd like some gas/oil/water
Wó xiăng yào qìyóu/jīyóu/shŭi
我想要汽油／机油／水

Will you drive us around today?
Jīntiān nǐ néng kāichē dài wǒmen chūqù ma?
今天你能开车带我们出去吗？

I'd like to rent a car
Wó xiăng zū yíliàng chē
我想租一辆车

How much will it cost?
Yào duōshăo qián?
要多少钱？

How much is it per kilometer?
Měi gōnglǐ yào dūo shăo qián?
每公里要多少钱？

Please stop here
Qĭng zài zhèlĭ tíng yíxià
请在这里停一下

Please wait here for . . . minutes
Qĭng zài zhèlĭ dĕng . . . fēnzhōng
请在这里等...分钟

Please drive to . . .
Qíng bă chē kāi dào . . .
请把车开到...

SOME COMMON ROAD SIGNS

此路不通	cǐ lù bù tōng	no through road
单行线	dānxíngxiàn	one-way street
禁止超车	jìnzhǐ chāo chē	no passing
禁止鸣笛	jìnzhǐ míngdí	do not sound vehicle horn
禁止停车	jìnzhǐ tíng chē	no parking
禁止通行	jìnzhǐ tōngxíng	road closed
慢	màn	slow
前方施工	qiánfāng shīgōng	road work
让	ràng	yield
人行道	rénxíngdào	pedestrians
人行横道	rénxínghéngdào	pedestrian crossing
危险	wēixiǎn	danger
小心	xiǎoxīn	caution
注意行人	zhùyì xíngrén	beware of pedestrians

THINGS YOU'LL SEE

柴油	cháiyóu	diesel
汽油	qìyóu	gas
加油站	jiāyóuzhàn	gas station
车库	chēkù	garage

THINGS YOU'LL HEAR

zhào zhí zǒu	straight ahead
zài zuǒ biān	on the left
xiàng zuó guǎi	turn left
zài yòu biān	on the right
xiàng yòu guǎi	turn right
kào yòu dì yī ge guǎi wān	first on the right
kào zuǒ dì èr ge gǔai wān	second on the left
guòle . . .	past the . . .

Kéyǐ kàn yíxià nǐde zhízhào ma?
May I see your license?

TRAIN TRAVEL

The Chinese train system is extensive and punctual, covering huge distances with little delay. However, the system is hopelessly overloaded and this means that it is very difficult to buy tickets.

First class, "soft sleeper" (*ruǎn wò*), is usually reserved for VIPs and foreigners, and consists of four-bed compartments. These are very luxurious, and each car has its own washroom and toilets. "Hard sleeper" (*yìngwò*) is second class with sixty berths to a car. There is a long open corridor down one side of the car and berths are grouped in sections of two tiers of three. This is the most popular way to travel and consequently the hardest type of ticket to buy. Third class, "hard seat" (*yìng zuò*), can be compared to traveling in a sardine can.

Passengers boarding mid-route are usually unable to buy a seat ticket, so they stand throughout their trip. The car can become extremely overcrowded. Hard seat tickets are, however, very inexpensive and the easiest tickets to buy.

There are no round trip tickets in China and tickets can only be bought at the point of departure not more than three days in advance. To avoid the long lines at the train stations, you should try to buy your ticket through CITS, although bookings must be made at least five days in advance.

Once on the train, there is a restaurant car, which serves three meals a day, and a snack cart service. In both cases, meal tickets should be bought in advance from a train employee who passes through the train. Food is also sold on every platform throughout the trip. Each train has at least one water boiler that supplies the only water suitable for drinking on the train.

It is often possible, with a lot of persistence, to upgrade a ticket once on the train. Each train has an office for this purpose, but you need to be quite determined to do it—being pleasant and friendly is usually far more effective than losing your temper!

USEFUL WORDS AND PHRASES

attendant	lièchēyuán	列车员
baggage rack	xínglǐ jià	行李架
baggage storage office	xínglǐ jìcún chù	行李寄存处
boiled water	kāishuǐ	开水
connection	zhōngzhuǎn	中转
dining car	cānchē	餐车
emergency applied brake	jǐnjí zhìdòngzhá	紧急制动闸
entrance	rùkǒu	入口
exit	chūkǒu	出口
first class (*soft sleeper*)	ruǎnwò	软卧
get in	shàngchē	上车
get out	xiàchē	下车
guard	liè chē zhǎng	列车长
lost and found	shīwù zhāolǐng	失物招领
platform	zhàntái	站台
platform ticket	zhàntái piào	站台票
railroad	tiělù	铁路
reservation office	shòupiàochù	售票处
seat	zuòwèi	座位
second class (*hard sleeper*)	yìngwò	硬卧
single ticket	dānchéng piào	单程票
soft seat	ruǎnzuò	软座
station	huǒchēzhàn	火车站

station master	zhànzhǎng	站长
third class *(hard seat)*	yìngzuò	硬座
ticket	chēpiào	车票
timetable	lièchē shíkè biǎo	列车时刻表
train	huǒchē	火车
waiting room	hòuchēshì	候车室

When does the train for . . . leave?
Qù . . . de huǒchē jídiǎn chūfā?
去...的火车几点出发?

When is the next train to . . .?
Qù . . . de xiàyítàng chē shì jídiǎn?
去...的下一趟车是几点?

When is the first train to . . .?
Qù . . . de tóubānchē shì jídiǎn?
去...的头班车是几点?

When is the last train to . . .?
Qù . . . de mòbānchē shì jídiǎn?
去...的末班车是几点?

How much is the fare to . . .?
Qù . . . de chēpiào duōshǎo qián?
去...的车票多少钱?

Do I have to change?
Wǒ yào huàn chē ma?
我要换车吗?

I want to change my ticket to a hard sleeper/soft sleeper
Wó xiǎng bá wǒde piào huànchéng yìngwò /ruǎnwò
我想把我的票换成硬卧／软卧

I want to buy a hard seat ticket
Wó xiáng mǎi yìzhāng yìngzuò piào
我想买一张硬座票

How long does it take to get to . . .?
Dào . . . qù yào duōcháng shíjiān?
到...去要多长时间?

A ticket to . . . please
Qíng mǎi yìzhāng qù . . . de piào
请买一张去...的票

Is this the right train for . . .?
Zhè shì qù . . . de huǒchē ma?
这是去...的火车吗

Is this the right platform for the . . . train?
Qù . . . shì cōng zhège zhàntái shàngchē ma?
去...是从这个站台上车吗?

Which platform for the . . . train?
Qù . . . shì jǐ hào zhàntái?
去...是几号站台?

Is this seat free?
Zhège wèizi yǒurén ma?
这个位子有人吗?

This seat is taken
Zhège wèizi yǐjīng yǒurén le
这个位子已经有人了

Can I change to the bottom/middle/top bunk?
Wǒ néng bù néng huàn dào xiàpù/zhōngpù/shàngpù?
我能不能换到下铺／中铺／上铺?

Can I shut/open the curtains?
Wǒ kéyǐ lāshàng/lākāi chuānglián ma?
我可以拉上／拉开窗帘吗?

Where is the boiled water?
Kāishuǐ zài nálǐ?
开水在哪里?

Where is the restroom?
Cèsuǒ zài nálǐ?
厕所在哪里?

May I open/close the window?
Wǒ kéyǐ kāichuāng/guānchuāng ma?
我可以开／关窗吗?

When do we arrive in . . .?
Wǒmen shénme shí hòu dàodá . . .?
我们什么时候到达...?

What station is this?
Zhè shì shénme zhàn?
这是什么站?

Do we stop at . . .?
Wǒmen zài . . . tíng ma?
我们在...停吗?

Would you keep an eye on my things for a moment?
Qǐng nǐ bāng wǒ kān yīhuir dōngxi, hǎo ma?
请你帮我看一会儿东西，好吗?

Is there a restaurant car on this train?
Zhè tàng chē shàng yǒu cānchē ma?
这趟车上有餐车吗？

THINGS YOU'LL SEE

厕所	cèsuǒ	restroom
出口	chūkǒu	exit
候车室	hòuchēshì	waiting room
禁止入内	jìnzhǐ rù nèi	no entry
禁止吸烟	jìnzhǐ xīyān	no smoking
开水	kāishuǐ	boiled water
冷水	léngshuǐ	cold water
全国铁路示意图	quánguó tiělù shìyì tú	All-China railroad map
热水	rèshuǐ	hot water
入口	rùkǒu	entrance
售票处	shòupiào chù	ticket office
问讯处	wènxùnchù	information
无人	wúrén	vacant
行李寄存处	xínglǐ jìcún chù	baggage storage
洗手间	xíshǒujiān	washroom
站台	zhàntái	platform
站台票	zhàntái piào	platform ticket

THINGS YOU'LL HEAR

Lǚkèmen zhùyì
Attention all passengers

. . . zhàn bù tíng
does not stop in . . .

Chápiào/Jiǎnpiào
Tickets, please

Qǐng qǐlái, huàn chuángdān le
Please get up, we want to change the sheets

Háiyǒu . . . fēnzhōng, lièchē jiù dàodá . . . zhàn le
We arrive in (place) . . . in (time) . . .

Qǐng lǚkèmen jiǎnchá yíxià zìjǐ de xínglǐ
Please check that you have all your baggage with you

Zhù dàjiā lǚtú yúkuài
We wish everyone a pleasant trip

AIR TRAVEL

Many international airlines fly to several destinations within China, and, in recent years, the number of international connections has increased considerably. Within China there are some fourteen local airlines, overseen by the CAAC (Civil Aviation Administration of China). The system of internal flights is extensive and reasonably efficient. Reserving tickets through local CAAC offices, hotel desks, and travel agents is relatively easy. Although it can sometimes be difficult to buy tickets for a few days ahead, they can be reserved, free of charge, for a flight a few weeks ahead.

Foreigners usually have to pay a large surcharge, which makes their tickets considerably more expensive than those of Chinese travelers. There is also a departure tax.

USEFUL WORDS AND PHRASES

aircraft	fēijī	飞机
airline	hángkōng gōngsī	航空公司
airport	jīchǎng	机场
airport shuttle	jīchǎng bānchē	机场班车
arrival	dàodá	到达
baggage cart	xínglǐchē	行李车
baggage claim	xínglǐ tíqǔ chù	行李提取处
boarding card	dēngjī pái	登机牌
check in (*verb*)	bànlǐ dēngjī shǒuxù	办理登机手续
customs	hǎiguān	海关
delay	wándiǎn	晚点
departure	qǐfēi	起飞
departure lounge	hòujīshì	候机室
emergency exit	ānquánmén	安全门

flight	hángbān	航班
flight attendant (*f.*)	kōngzhōng xiáojiě	空中小姐
flight attendant (*f.*)	nǔ fúwùyuán	女服务员
flight attendant (*m.*)	nán fúwùyuán	男服务员
flight number	hángbān hào	航班号
gate	dēngjīkǒu	登机口
passport	hùzhào	护照
seat	zuòwèi	座位
seat belt	ānquándài	安全带

When is there a flight to . . .?
Qù . . . de hángbān shì jídiǎn?
去...的航班是几点?

What time does the flight to . . . leave?
Qù . . . de hángbān jídián qǐfēi?
去...的航班几点起飞?

Is it a direct flight?
Zhè shì zhídá hángbān ma?
这是直达航班吗?

Do I have to change planes?
Wǒ xūyào huàn jī ma?
我需要换机吗?

When do I have to check in?
Jí diǎnzhōng bànlǐ dēngjī shǒuxù?
几点钟办理登机手续?

I'd like a ticket to . . .
Wó xiǎngyào yìzhāng qù . . . de jīpiào
我想要一张去...的机票

I'd like a nonsmoking seat, please
Wó xiǎngyào yíge jìnyānqū de zuòwèi
我想要一个禁烟区的座位

I'd like a window seat, please
Wó xiǎngyào yíge kào chuāng de zuòwèi
我想要一个靠窗的座位

How long will the flight be delayed?
Zhège hángbān jiāng wándiǎn duōjiǔ?
这个航班将晚点多久?

Which gate for the flight to . . .?
Qù . . . de hángbān zài nǎge dēngjīkǒu?
去...的航班在哪个登机口?

When do we arrive in . . .?
Wǒmen jí diǎnzhōng dàodá . . .?
我们几点钟到达...?

May I smoke now?
Wǒ xiànzài kéyǐ xīyān ma?
我现在可以吸烟吗?

I don't feel very well
Wó gǎnjué bù shūfú
我感觉不舒服

Do you have any more tickets for . . .?
Háiyǒu qù . . . de jīpiào ma?
还有去...的机票吗?

I want to join the standby line for today's flight to . . .
Wó xiáng děng jīntiān qù . . . de hòubǔ jīpiào
我想等今天去...的候补机票

THINGS YOU'LL SEE

安全门	ānquánmén	emergency exit
办理登机手续	bànlǐ dēngjī shǒuxù	check-in
乘客	chéngkè	passengers
出口	chūkǒu	exit
当地时间	dāngdì shíjiān	local time
到达	dàodá	arrivals
登机口	dēngjīkǒu	gate
国际航线	guójì hángxiàn	international airline
国内航线	guónèi hángxiàn	domestic airline
海关检查	hǎiguān jiǎnchá	customs
航班	hángbān	flight
护照检查	hùzhào jiǎnchá	passport control
系好安全带	jì hǎo ānquán dài	fasten seat belt
紧急降落	jǐnjí jiàngluò	emergency landing
禁烟区	jìnyānqū	nonsmokers
旅客	lǚkè	passengers
免税商店	miǎnshuì shāngdiàn	duty-free shop
起飞	qǐfēi	departures
请不要吸烟	qǐng búyào xīyān	no smoking please
入口	rùkǒu	entrance
问讯处	wènxùnchù	information
行李提取处	xínglǐ tíqǔ chù	baggage claim
预定航班	yùdìng hángbān	scheduled flight

→

直达航班	**zhídá hángbān**	direct flight
中国民航	**Zhōngguó Mínháng**	CAAC (Civil Aviation Administration of China)

THINGS YOU'LL HEAR

Qù . . . de hángbān xiànzài kāishǐ dēngjī
The flight for . . . is now boarding

Xiànzài qǐng qù . . . hào dēngjīkǒu
Please go now to gate number . . .

Qù . . . de hángbān wándiǎn le
The flight to . . . is delayed

BUS, BOAT, AND CITY TRANSPORTATION

In towns and cities there is usually a good bus service, although the buses do tend to stop running rather early (around 11 PM). Route maps can be bought on the street from hawkers. Tickets are very inexpensive and are bought from the conductor on the bus. Inexpensive monthly tickets for unlimited use within a given area are available from the bus company. Buses tend to be very overcrowded, particularly during the rush hour, since there is no limit to the number of passengers allowed. So be prepared to elbow your way on!

There is also an extensive bus service between towns, although buses don't always stop in the countryside or in small villages to pick up passengers. Travel is usually slow and conditions often crowded, but, for shorter journeys, buses can be a fairly pleasant way to travel in China. One-way tickets, which are not expensive, can be bought at the bus station you are leaving from no more than three days in advance, but return tickets are not available. It is usually reasonably easy to buy bus tickets. Different prices for the same destination indicate the quality of the bus, and it is often advisable to spend a little more on your ticket. On a trip of two or more days, the bus will pull in to a youth hostel-type hotel in the evening. The cost of the overnight stay is not included in the ticket. Buses leave early and promptly the next day, often without waiting for late risers.

There are modern subway systems in central Beijing and Shanghai, with tickets costing just a few "*jiao.*" Within cities, the fastest way to travel is by taxi. These can be ordered from hotels or outside tourist sights, or hailed on the street. In tourist centers it is usually possible to rent a minibus from hotels for sight-seeing tours.

On navigable rivers there are usually ferries. However, the standard varies, depending on how remote the area is. Large ferries, such as those plying the Changjiang River (Yangtse) or those going to and from Hainan Island, have five classes of accommodations. First class is extremely luxurious, second is a four-berth cabin, third class is a dormitory-type cabin for 8–10 people, fourth class is a large public cabin, and fifth class is floor space in the hold. Food on board tends to be bad, so it is advisable to take some of your own. There are also pleasant, inexpensive evening ferries between Hong Kong and Guangzhou, and this is often the easiest way to travel this route.

USEFUL WORDS AND PHRASES

adult	dàrén/chéngnián rén	大人 / 成年人
boat	chuán	船
bus	gōnggòng qìchē	公共汽车
bus *(in town)*	shìqūchē	市区车
(suburbs)	jiāoqūchē	郊区车
(long distance)	chángtú qìchē	长途汽车
bus station	qìchē zǒng zhàn	汽车总站
bus stop	qìchē zhàn	汽车站
child	értóng	儿童
conductor	shòupiàoyuán	售票员
connection	liányùn	联运
cruise boat	yóuchuán	游船
driver	sījī	司机
fare	chēfèi	车费
ferry	dùchuán	渡船
long-distance bus	lǚyóu chē	旅游车
minibus	xiǎo gōnggòng qìchē	小公共汽车
monthly ticket	yuèpiào	月票
night bus	yèbānchē	夜班车
number 5 bus	wǔ lù gōnggòng qìchē	5 路公共汽车
passenger	chéngkè	乘客

pier	mǎtóu	码头
port	gángkǒu	港口
river	jiāng/hé	江／河
sea	hǎi	海
seat	zuòwèi	座位
station (*long-distance bus*)	chángtú chēzhàn	长途汽车站
station (*town bus*)	qìchē zǒng zhàn	汽车总站
station (*subway*)	dì tiě zhàn	地铁站
subway	dìtiě	地铁
taxi	chūzūchē	出租车
ticket	chēpiào	车票
transit system map	jiāotōngtú	交通图

Where is the bus station?
Qìchē zǒngzhàn zài nálǐ?
汽车总站在哪里？

Where is there a bus stop?
Nálǐ yǒu qìchē zhàn?
哪里有汽车站？

Where is the number 5 bus stop?
Wǔ lù qìchē zhàn zài nálǐ?
5 路汽车站在哪里？

Which buses go to . . .?
Qù . . . zuò jǐ lù chē?
去...坐几路车？

How often do the buses to . . . run?
Qù . . . de chē duō cháng shíjiān yítàng?
去...的车多长时间一趟?

Where is the nearest subway station?
Nǎge dìtiě zhàn zuì jìn?
最近的地铁站在哪里?

Would you tell me when we get to . . .?
Nǐ néng bù néng dào . . . zhàn jiào wǒ yíxià?
到...站时你能不能叫我一下?

Do I have to get off yet?
Wǒ zài zhèlǐ xiàchē ma?
我在这里下车吗?

How do you get to . . .?
Qù . . . zénme zǒu?
去...怎么走?

Is it very far?
Hén yuǎn ma?
很远吗?

I'd like to go to . . .
Wó xiǎng qù . . .
我想去...

Do you go near . . .?
Nǐ qù . . . fùjìn ma?
你去...附近吗?

Where can I buy a ticket?
Zài nálǐ mǎi piào?
在哪里买票?

Could you open/close the window?
Nǐ néng bù néng kāi/guān yíxia chuāng?
你能不能开 / 关一下窗?

Could you help me get a ticket?
Nǐ néng bù néng bāng wó mǎi zhāng piào?
你能不能帮我买一张票?

When does the last bus leave?
Mòbān chē shì jídiǎn?
末班车是几点?

When does the first bus leave?
Tóubān chē shì jídiǎn?
头班车是几点?

THINGS YOU'LL SEE

保持车内清洁	bǎochí chē nèi qīngjié	keep the bus clean
查票员	chápiàoyuán	ticket inspector
出口	chūkǒu	exit
出租汽车站	chūzū qìchē zhàn	taxi stand
后门	hòumén	entry at the rear
加班车	jiāchē	extra service (rush hour)
禁止入内	jìnzhǐ rù nèi	no entry
开车时间	kāichē shíjiān	departure
快车	kuàichē	express bus

→

老、幼、病、残、 孕专座	lǎo, yòu, bìng, cán, yùn, zhuānzuò	seats for the elderly, children, the sick, the disabled, and pregnant women
路线	lùxiàn	route
码头	mǎtóu	harbor
前门	qiánmén	entry at the front
请勿随地吐痰	qǐng wù suídì tǔtán	no spitting
请勿吸烟	qǐng wù xīyān	no smoking
请勿与司机谈话	qǐng wù yǔ sījī tánhuà	do not speak to the driver
区间车	qūjiānchē	shuttle bus (only going part of route)
入口	rùkǒu	entrance
售票处	shòupiàochù	ticket office
司机	sījī	driver
太平门	tàipíngmén	emergency exit
停	tíng	stop
先下后上	xiān xià hòu shàng	allow passengers to get off before boarding
小心扒手	xiǎoxīn páshǒu	beware of pickpockets
终点站	zhōngdiǎnzhàn	terminal
中门	zhōngmén	entry at the middle

BICYCLES

The most practical and pleasant way to travel short distances in China is by bicycle. Bicycles tend to be heavy and gearless but solid and quite fast on flat ground. They can be rented from most tourist hotels and also privately, although prices vary considerably. There are bike repairers—who will also pump up tires—on many street corners. They usually do a fast, effective, and inexpensive job. Chinese people often bike very slowly, with little apparent control, but, after a while, it is easy to get used to the crowded biking conditions. Ride on the right. Traffic coming onto a traffic circle has priority. If you are turning right at traffic lights, you just continue and do not have to stop at the lights. In towns and cities, bicycles should be parked in designated lots for bicycles. A small fee is charged for parking.

USEFUL WORDS AND PHRASES

basket	kuāng	筐
bell	chēlíng	车铃
bicycle	zìxíngchē	自行车
brakes	shāchē	刹车
chain	liàntiáo	链条
flat tire	chuānkǒng	穿孔
handlebars	chēbǎ	车把
inner tube	nèitāi	内胎
lock	suǒ	锁
man's bicycle	nánchē	男车
pedal	tàjiǎo	踏脚
pump	dǎqìtǒng	打气筒
rent	zū	租
seat	ānzuò	鞍座

spoke	(lún)fú	（轮）辐
tire	chētāi	车胎
tricycle	sānlúnchē	三轮车
wheel	chēlún	车轮
women's bicycle	nǚchē	女车

I'd like to rent a bicycle
Wǒ xiǎng zū yíliàng zìxíngchē
我想租一辆自行车

How much does it cost for one hour/day?
Méi xiǎoshí/měitiān duōshǎo qián?
每小时 / 每天多少钱？

Do you need a deposit?
Xūyào fù yājīn ma?
需要付押金吗？

Could you please fix this flat tire?
Qǐng bǔ yíxia chētāi
请补一下车胎

Could you please fix the brakes?
Qǐng xiū yíxia shāchē
请修一下刹车

Could you pump up the tires for me?
Qǐng nǐ bāng wǒ dǎ yíxia qì, hǎo ma?
请你帮我打一下气，好吗？

Where can I park the bicycle?
Nálǐ kéyǐ tíngfàng zìxíngchē?
哪里可以停放自行车？

How much does it cost to park the bicycle?
Cúnchē yào duōshǎo qián?
存车要多少钱?

Could you raise/lower the seat?
Nǐ néng bù néng bāng wǒ bǎ chēzuò fàng gāo/fàng dī yīxiē?
你能不能帮我把车座放高／放低一些?

THINGS YOU'LL SEE

出租自行车	chūzū zìxíngchē	bicycle rental
存车处	cúnchē chù	bike parking lot
骑车不准带人	qíchē bùzhǔn dài rén	carrying passengers on a bicycle is not allowed
修理自行车	xiūlǐ zìxíngchē	bicycle repairs
自行车道	zìxíngchē dào	bike lane
自行车存放处	zìxíngchē cúnfàng chù	bike parking lot

DOING BUSINESS

Doing business in China is often a painfully slow and frustrating experience for Western companies used to quick decisions. In China, politics, economics, and business are inseparable and industry is very hierarchical. Factories or companies are usually responsible to the relevant provincial-level ministry, but exceptionally large or important factories may have to report directly to the relevant ministry in Beijing. Chinese industry is undergoing a program of decentralization, but this is taking some time. Meanwhile, the hierarchical setup inevitably means that decision-making is lengthy, because any plan agreed to at the local level must also be agreed to, and often altered, at the provincial and national levels. However, foreign companies trading in China are advised to have direct involvement with the central authorities because their approval gives a measure of protection.

Most ministries, corporations, and large factories can provide their own English interpreters, who usually have a good technical background.

When approaching any level of authority, it is very important to take your business card, clearly stating your position in your company, since status is considered very important. Laying the groundwork for any type of business deal will involve banquets and speeches. If the Chinese hosts invite the Western company to a banquet, it is considered polite for the company's representatives to then host a return banquet a few days later. During a banquet there are always speeches, made by both sides. It is advisable to stress the importance of international friendship and cooperation and mutual assistance. Banquets often involve drinking a lot of "*máotái*"—a Chinese liquor. Be careful of the alcohol content of this drink!

USEFUL WORDS AND PHRASES

accept	jiēshòu	接受
accountant	kuàiji	会计

accounting department	cáiwù kē	财务科
advertisement	guǎnggào	广告
advertising	guǎnggào	广告
air freight (*verb*)	kōngyùn	空运
bid	tóubiāo	投标
board (*of directors*)	dǒngshìhuì	董事会
brochure	xiǎocèzi	小册子
business card	míngpiàn	名片
businessman	shāngrén	商人
chairman (*of company*)	zhǔguǎn/zǒngcái	主管 / 总裁
company	gōngsī	公司
computer	jìsuànjī/diànnǎo	计算机 / 电脑
consumer	xiāofèizhě	消费者
contract	hétóng	合同
cost	chéngběn	成本
customer	gùkè/kèhù	顾客 / 客户
director	dǒngshì	董事
discount	jiǎnjià	减价
documents	wénjiàn	文件
down payment	dìngjīn	订金
engineer	gōngchéngshī	工程师
executive	dǒngshì	董事
expensive	guì	贵
exports	chūkǒu shāngpǐn	出口商品
fax	chuánzhēn	传真

import (*verb*)	jìnkǒu	进口
imports	jìnkǒu shāngpǐn	进口商品
inexpensive	piányi	便宜
installment	fēnqī fùkuǎn	分期付款
invoice (*noun*)	fāpiào	发票
invoice (*verb*)	kāi fāpiào	开发票
leader	lǐngdǎo	领导
letter	xìn	信
letter of credit	xìnyòng zhèng	信用证
loss	kuīsǔn	亏损
manager	jīnglǐ	经理
manufacture	zhìzào	制造
margin	chā é	差额
market	shìchǎng	市场
marketing	shìchǎng yíngxiāo	市场营销
meeting	huìyì	会议
negotiations	tánpàn	谈判
offer (*quote*)	bàojià	报价
order (*noun*)	dìnghuò dān	订货单
order (*verb*)	dìnghuò	订货
personnel	zhíyuán	职员
price	jiàgé	价格
product	chánpǐn	产品
production	shēngchǎn	生产
profit	lìrùn	利润
promotion (*publicity*)	xuānchuán	宣传

purchase order	gòuhuò dìngdān	购货订单
sales department	xiāoshònbù	销售部
sales director	yíngyè zhǔrèn	营业主任
sales figures	xiāoshòu'é	销售额
secretary	mìshū	秘书
shipment	zhuāngyùn	装运
tax	shuì	税
telex	diànchuán	电传
tender (*noun*)	tóubiāo	投标
total	zǒng'é	总额

My name is . . .
Wǒ jiào . . .
我叫...

Here's my card
Zhèshì wǒde míngpiàn
这是我的名片

Pleased to meet you
Hěn gāoxìng rènshì nǐ
很高兴认识你

May I introduce . . .?
Wǒ lái jièshào yíxià . . .
我来介绍一下...

My company is . . .
Wǒde gōngsī jiào . . .
我的公司叫...

Our product is selling very well in the US market
Wǒmen de chánpǐn zài Měiguó shìchǎng xiāolù hén hǎo
我们的产品在美国市场销路很好

We are looking for partners in China
Wǒmen zhèng zài Zhōngguó xúnzhǎo màoyì huǒbàn
我们正在中国寻找贸易伙伴

At our last meeting . . .
Zài wǒmen shàngcì kāihuì shí . . .
在我们上次开会时...

10 percent/25 percent/50 percent
Bǎi fēn zhī shí/bǎi fēn zhī èrshíwǔ/bǎi fēn zhī wǔshí
百分之十 / 百分之二十五 / 百分之五十

More than . . .
Bǐ . . . duō
比...多

Less than . . .
Bǐ . . . shǎo
比...少

We're on schedule
Wǒmen shì ànshí de
我们是按时的

We're slightly behind schedule
Wǒmen bǐ yùdìng jìhuà wǎnle yìdiǎn
我们比预定计划晚了一点

Please accept our apologies
Qǐng jiēshòu wǒmen de dàoqiàn
请接受我们的道歉

There are good government grants available
Néng dédào xiāngdāng dūo de zhèngfǔ zīzhù
能得到相当多的政府资助

It's a deal
Zhèyàng jiù suàn chéngjiāo le
这样就算成交了

I'll have to check that with my chairman
Wǒ bìxū yú wǒmen huìzhǎng héduì yíxià nèige shìqíng
我必须与我们会长核对一下那个事情

I'll get back to you on that
Wǒ huító zài gàosù nǐ nèige
我回头再告诉你那个

Our quote will be with you very shortly
Wǒmen de bàojià hěnkuǎi jiù huì géi nǐmen
我们的报价很快就会给你们

We'll send it by telex
Wǒmen huì dǎ diànchuán de
我们会打电传的

We'll send them air freight
Wǒmen huì kōngyùn de
我们会空运的

It's a pleasure to do business with you
Wǒmen hěn gāoxìng yú nǐmen yìqǐ zuò shēngyì
我们很高兴与你们一起做生意

We look forward to a mutually beneficial business relationship
Wǒmen qídài zhe yú nǐmen jiànlì yìzhǒng hùlì de màoyì guānxì
我们期待着与你们建立一种互利的贸易关系

RESTAURANTS

Joint-venture hotels have good international cuisine with excellent service at international prices. Good Chinese hotels also provide meals, paid for separately from the cost of a room —although standards vary. It is, however, much less expensive and often more interesting to eat in one of the many Chinese restaurants. Chinese restaurants are rarely as clean as Western ones, but don't be put off too easily. If lots of Chinese people are eating there, it probably serves good food. Don't worry about language shortcomings: it's perfectly acceptable to walk into the kitchen and point to whatever you would like to eat. All meals are served with rice and usually with tea. There will be large thermos flasks of boiled water available to refill your cup of tea. Most restaurants sell beer and "*báijiǔ*," the fiery Chinese liquor.

It is not customary to tip, either in restaurants or in hotels. Chinese people eat with chopsticks, but a spoon can be provided on request.

There is little similarity between Chinese food in the US and Chinese food in China, since much of the food available in the US tends to be Cantonese food adapted for the American palate. Food in China varies a great deal between regions and seasons, so it is hard to generalize about flavor. If possible, try local specialties. A Chinese meal rarely includes dessert and usually finishes with soup. Note that Chinese people often eat their rice last. So, if you want rice to accompany the meal, it may be necessary to ask for it specially.

Useful Words and Phrases

beer	píjiǔ	啤酒
bill	zhàngdān	帐单
bottle	píngzi	瓶子
bowl	wǎn	碗
chopsticks	kuàizi	筷子

coffee	kāfēi	咖啡
cup	bēizi	杯子
fork	chāzi	叉子
glass	bōlibēi	玻璃杯
hot (*spicy*)	là	辣
knife	dāo	刀
menu	càidān	菜单
milk	niúnǎi	牛奶
napkin	cānjīn	餐巾
plate	pánzi	盘子
rice	mǐfàn	米饭
sandwich	sānmíngzhì	三明治
snack	diǎnxīn	点心
soup	tāng	汤
soy sauce	jiàngyóu	酱油
spoon	tiáogēng	调羹
sugar	táng	糖
table	zhuōzi	桌子
tea	chá	茶
teahouse	cháguǎn	茶馆
teaspoon	cháchí	茶匙
waiter	nán fúwùyuán	男服务员
waitress	nǔ fúwùyuán	女服务员
water	shuǐ	水
wine	jiǔ	酒

A table for two, please
Qǐng yào yìzhāng liǎngge rén de zhuōzi
请要一张两个人的桌子

May I see the menu?
Wǒ néng kàn yíxia càidān ma?
我能看一下菜单吗?

I'd like . . .
Wó xiǎngyào . . .
我想要...

Just a cup of tea, please
Jiù yào yìbēi chá
就要一杯茶

Waiter/waitress!
Fúwùyuán!
服务员!

May we pay, please?
Fùkuǎn
付款

Not too hot (spicy), please
Qǐng búyào tài là
请不要太辣

I didn't order this
Wǒ méiyǒu diǎn zhège
我没有点这个

May we have some more . . .?
Wǒmen kéyǐ zài yào yíxie . . . ma?
我们可以再要一些...吗?

That was excellent, thank you
Zhè dùn fàn tài hǎo chīle, xièxiè nǐ
这顿饭太好吃了，谢谢你

I can't use chopsticks
Wǒ búhuì yòng kuàizi
我不会用筷子

Do you cook with pork fat?
Nǐmen shì bú shì yòng zhūyóu shāo de?
你们是不是用猪油烧的？

I only want vegetables
Wó zhǐ yào shūcài
我只要蔬菜

I am a vegetarian
Wǒ shì chīsù de
我是吃素的

THINGS YOU'LL HEAR

Ní xiǎng chīdiǎn shénme?
What would you like?

Nǐ huì yòng kuàizi ma?
Can you use chopsticks?

Nǐ chī làjiāo ma?
Do you eat chili?

THINGS YOU'LL SEE

菜单	càidān	menu
菜馆	càiguǎn	restaurant
餐馆	cāguǎn	restaurant
茶馆	cháguǎn	teahouse (large)
茶室	cháshì	teahouse (smaller)
饭店	fàndiàn	restaurant
饭庄	fànzhuāng	restaurant
糕点店	gāodiǎndiàn	pastry shop
今日供应	jīnrì gōngyìng	today's menu
酒家	jiǔjiā	restaurant
酒楼	jiǔlóu	restaurant
咖啡店	kāfēidiàn	coffee shop
快餐店	kuàicāndiàn	fast food
冷饮店	léngyǐndiàn	cold drinks bar
奶制品店	nǎi zhìpǐn diàn	dairy products café (sells milk, yogurt, ice cream, pastries, cookies, etc.)
清真饭店	qīngzhēn fàndiàn	Muslim restaurant
收款台	shōukuǎntái	cashier
素菜馆	sùcàiguǎn	vegetarian restaurant
小吃店	xiǎochīdiàn	snackbar
西餐厅	xīcāntīng	Western-style restaurant
饮食店	yǐnshídiàn	café

MENU GUIDE

RICE AND NOODLES

炒饭	chǎofàn	fried rice
炒面	chǎomiàn	fried noodles
炒米粉	cháomǐfěn	fried rice noodles
蛋炒饭	dàn chǎofàn	fried rice with egg
面条	miàntiáo	noodles
米饭	mǐfàn	rice
糯米	nuòmǐ	glutinous rice
稀饭	xīfàn	rice porridge, congee

SOME BASIC FOOD ITEMS

春卷	chūnjuǎn	spring rolls
豆沙包	dòushābāo	steamed dumplings with sweet bean paste filling
花卷	huājuǎn	steamed rolls
馒头	mántou	steamed bread
面包	miànbāo	bread (white)
奶酪	nǎilào	cheese
肉	ròu	meat (usually pork)
咸菜	xiáncài	pickles

COOKING METHODS AND BASIC COMBINATIONS

炒...	chǎo . . .	stir-fried . . .
叉烧...	chāshāo . . .	barbecued . . .
...丁	. . . dīng	diced . . .

各菇...	**dōnggū** . . .	. . . with dried mushrooms
咖喱...	**gālí** . . .	curried . . .
宫保...	**gōngbǎo** . . .	stir-fried . . . with peanuts and chili
蚝油...	**háoyóu** . . .	. . . with oyster sauce
红烧...	**hóngshāo** . . .	. . . braised in brown sauce
滑溜...	**huáliū** . . .	stir-fried . . . with sauce added
烩...	**huì** . . .	stewed . . .
火锅...	**huǒguō** . . .	. . . in hotpot
火腿...	**huótuǐ** . . .	. . . with ham
家常...	**jiācháng** . . .	home-style . . .
烤...	**kǎo** . . .	roasted . . .
...块	. . . **kuài**	. . . chunks, pieces
辣子...	**làzi** . . .	. . . with chili
麻酱...	**májiàng** . . .	. . . quick-fried in sesame paste
麻辣...	**málà** . . .	. . . with chili and wild pepper
...片	. . . **piàn**	sliced . . .
茄汁...	**qiézhī** . . .	. . . with tomato sauce
清蒸...	**qīngzhēng** . . .	steamed . . .
三鲜...	**sānxiān** . . .	"three-fresh" . . . (with three varied ingredients)
...丝	. . . **sī**	shredded . . .

糖醋...	tángcù . . .	sweet and sour . . .
...丸（元）	. . . wán (or yuán)	. . . balls
香酥...	xiāngsū . . .	crispy deep-fried . . .
炸...	zhá . . .	deep-fried . . .
榨菜...	zhàcài . . .	. . . with pickled mustard greens
蒸...	zhēng . . .	steamed . . .

PORK

叉烧肉	chāshāo ròu	barbecued pork
辣子肉丁	làzi ròudīng	stir-fried diced pork with chili
米粉蒸肉	mǐfěn zhēngròu	steamed pork with rice
木须炒肉	mùxū chǎoròu	stir-fried sliced pork with eggs, tree-ear (edible fungus), and day lily (type of dried lily)
青椒炒肉片	qīngjiāo chǎo ròupiàn	stir-fried sliced pork with pepper
笋炒肉片	sún chǎo ròupiàn	stir-fried sliced pork with bamboo shoots
糖醋排骨	tángcù páigǔ	sweet and sour spareribs
榨菜炒肉丝	zhàcài chǎo ròusī	stir-fried shredded pork with pickled mustard greens
猪肉	zhūròu	pork

CHICKEN AND DUCK

白斩鸡	báizhǎnjī	sliced cold chicken
北京烤鸭	Běijīng kǎoyā	Peking duck
鸡	jī	chicken
酱爆鸡丁	jiàngbào jīdīng	diced chicken quick-fried with bean sauce
叫化鸡	jiàohuājī	"beggar's chicken" (charcoal-baked marinaded chicken)
鸡丁	jīdīng	diced chicken
香菇鸭掌	xiānggū yāzhǎng	duck's foot with mushroom
鸭	yā	duck

BEEF AND LAMB

葱爆牛肉	cōngbào niúròu	beef quick-fried with Chinese onions
宫保牛肉	gōngbǎo niúròu	stir-fried beef with peanuts and chili
红烧牛肉	hóngshāo niúròu	beef braised in brown sauce
烤羊肉串	kǎo yángròuchuàn	kabobs
牛肉	niúròu	beef
涮羊肉	shuàn yángròu	Mongolian hot-pot
羊肉	yángròu	lamb
鱼香牛肉	yúxiāng niúròu	stir-fried beef in hot spicy sauce

FISH AND SEAFOOD

芙蓉虾仁	**fúróng xiārén**	stir-fried shrimps with egg white
干烧黄鳝	**gānshāo huángshàn**	eel braised with chili and bean sauce
红烧鲤鱼	**hóngshāo lǐyú**	carp braised in brown sauce
滑溜鱼片	**huáliū yúpiàn**	stir-fried fish slices with thick sauce added
清蒸鲤鱼	**qīngzhēng lǐyú**	steamed carp
三丝鱼翅	**sānsī yúchì**	shark's fin with shredded sea cucumber, abalone, and bamboo shoots
糖醋鱼块	**tángcù yúkuài**	sweet and sour fish
虾	**xiā**	shrimps
鱿鱼	**yóuyú**	squid
鱼	**yú**	fish
鱼片	**yúpiàn**	fish slices

SPECIALTIES

包子	**bāozi**	steamed dumplings with minced pork or various fillings
叉烧包	**chāshāobāo**	steamed dumplings with barbecued pork filling
豆腐干	**dòufu gān**	dried bean curd

豆腐皮	**dòufu pí**	dried soy bean cream
腐竹	**fǔzhú**	"bean curd bamboo" (dried soy bean cream, in shape of bamboo)
锅巴豆腐	**guōbā dòufu**	bean curd fried in batter
锅贴	**guōtiē**	fried Chinese ravioli
馄饨	**húntun** (*or* **yúntún** *or* **chāoshǒu**)	small Chinese ravioli in soup
麻婆豆腐	**mápó dòufu**	"pock-marked woman bean curd" (bean curd with minced beef in hot spicy sauce)
三鲜豆腐	**sānxiān dòufu**	"three-fresh" bean curd (with three ingredients that vary)
水饺	**shuíjiǎo**	Chinese ravioli
松花蛋	**sōnghuādàn**	preserved eggs
馅饼	**xiànbǐng**	savory fritter
小笼包	**xiǎolóngbāo**	steamed dumplings with various fillings
虾仁豆腐	**xiārén dòufu**	bean curd with shrimps
油条	**yóutiáo**	unsweetened doughnut sticks
蒸饺	**zhēngjiǎo**	steamed Chinese ravioli

VEGETABLES

白菜	báicài	cabbage
菠菜	bōcài	spinach
炒豆芽	chǎo dòuyá	stir-fried bean sprouts
炒时菜	chǎo shícài	stir-fried seasonal vegetables
冬笋扁豆	dōngsún biǎndòu	stir-fried French beans with bamboo shoots
花菜	huācài	cauliflower
蘑菇	mógū	mushroom
茄子	qiézi	eggplant
素什锦	sù shíjǐn	stir-fried assorted vegetables
土豆	tǔdòu	potato
土豆条	tǔdòutiáo	French fries
鲜蘑豌豆	xiānmó wāndòu	stir-fried peas with mushrooms
西红柿	xīhóngshì	tomato
西红柿炒鸡蛋	xīhóngshì chǎo jīdàn	stir-fried tomato with egg
玉米	yùmǐ	corn

SOUPS

菠菜粉丝汤	**bōcài fěnsī tāng**	soup with spinach and vermicelli
三鲜汤	**sānxiān tāng**	"three-fresh" soup (normally shrimp, a meat, and a seasonal vegetable)
时菜肉片汤	**shícài ròupiàn tāng**	soup with sliced pork and seasonal vegetables
什锦冬瓜汤	**shíjǐn dōngguā tāng**	winter marrow soup
西红柿鸡蛋汤	**xīhóngshì jīdàn tāng**	soup with eggs and tomato
榨菜肉丝汤	**zhàcài ròusī tāng**	soup with shredded pork and pickled mustard greens
紫菜汤	**zǐcài tāng**	seaweed and dried shrimp soup

FRUIT

菠萝	**bōluó**	pineapple
广柑	**guǎnggān**	Guangdong sweet orange
哈密瓜	**hāmìguā**	honeydew melon
桔子（蜜桔）	**júzi** (*or* **mìjú**)	tangerine
梨	**lí**	pear
荔枝	**lìzhī**	litchi
苹果	**píngguǒ**	apple

葡萄	**pútao**	grape
香蕉	**xiāngjiāo**	banana
西瓜	**xīguā**	watermelon

DESSERTS

八宝饭	**bābǎo fàn**	"eight-treasure" rice desert (with eight types of fruit/nuts)
拨丝香蕉	**básī xiāngjiāo**	banana fritters
冰淇淋	**bīngqílín**	ice cream
冰糖银耳	**bīngtáng yín'ěr**	silver tree-ear in syrup (edible fungus)
什锦水果羹	**shíjǐn shuíguǒ gēng**	fruit salad soup
水果色拉	**shuíguǒ sèlā**	fruit salad

DRINKS

白酒	**báijiǔ**	baijiu (white liquor)
茶	**chá**	tea
咖啡	**kāfēi**	coffee
牛奶	**niúnǎi**	milk
啤酒	**píjiǔ**	beer
葡萄酒	**pútaojiǔ**	wine
汽水	**qìshuǐ**	lemonade

SHOPPING

If you are looking for presents and souvenirs to take home, large cities and tourist sites have "friendship stores" that sell a wide variety of national products as well as imported goods that may not be available elsewhere. Local crafts and antiques can also be found in specialized markets, as can silk and cashmere scarves, ties, and clothing, all at bargain prices if you are prepared for ruthless negotiation.

In larger towns and cities, stores are open from around 8 AM to 7 PM. You should buy things when you first see them, since they may be sold out if you go back a few days later. Each town has a "*bǎihùodàlóu*," a large department store, which usually sells just about everything. The larger cities now have some well-known Western chains and Japanese department stores, but these tend to be rather expensive. In many stores you will be given a price slip by the sales assistant, which you take and pay at another counter, then you take the receipt back to the original assistant to claim your purchase.

Shopping for food is best done in the daily open-air market, where fresh food is available at low prices, although there are considerable seasonal variations. Produce is bought in multiples of "*liǎng*" (100g), "*jīn*" (500g), and "*ōngjīn*" (1kg).

In the countryside, the small stores often sell very little other than the basic essentials and rather old candy and cookies.

USEFUL WORDS AND PHRASES

bookstore	shūdiàn	书店
butcher shop	ròudiàn	肉店
buy	mǎi	买
cash register	shōukuǎntái	收款台
department store	bǎihùodàlóu	百货大楼
drugstore	yàodiàn	药店
electrical store	diànqì shāngdiàn	电器商店

fashion	shízhuāng	时装
florist shop	huādiàn	花店
foreign language bookstore	wàiwén shūdiàn	外文书店
friendship store	yǒuyí shāngdiàn	友谊商店
general store	bǎihuòdiàn	百货店
hardware store	túchǎndiàn	土产店
inexpensive	piányi	便宜
market	càichǎng	菜场
menswear	nánzhuāng	男装
music store	yīnyùe shūdiàn	音乐书店
pastry shop	gāodiǎndiàn	糕点店
receipt	shōujù	收据
sale	jiǎnjià chūshòu	减价出售
sales assistant	shòuhuòyuán	售货员
shoe store	xiédiàn	鞋店
shop *(verb)*	qù mǎi dōngxi	去买东西
souvenir store	jìniàn pǐn shāngdiàn	纪念品商店
spend	huāfèi	花费
stationery store	wénjùdiàn	文具店
store *(noun)*	shāngdiàn	商店
supermarket	chāojí shìchǎng	超级市场
tailor's	cáifeng	裁缝
toystore	wánjùdiàn	玩具店
travel agency (CITS)	lǚxíngshè	旅行社
women's wear	nǚzhuāng	女装

I'd like . . .
Wó xiăngyào . . .
我想要…

Do you have . . .?
Nĭmen yŏu . . . ma?
你们有…吗?

How much is this?
Zhège duōshăo qián?
这个多少钱?

Where is the . . . department?
. . . bù zài nálĭ?
…部在哪里?

Do you have any more?
Hái yŏu ma?
还有吗?

I'd like to change this, please
Wó xiăngyào huàn zhège
我想要换这个

Do you have anything less expensive?
Hái yŏu gèng piányi de ma?
还有更便宜的吗?

Do you have anything larger?
Yŏu dà yìdiăn de ma?
有大一点的吗?

Do you have anything smaller?
Yóu xiăo yìdiăn de ma?
有小一点的吗?

Does it come in other colors?
Hái yǒu biéde yánsè ma?
还有别的颜色吗？

Could you wrap it for me?
Nǐ néng bù néng gěi wǒ bāo yíxià?
你能不能给我包一下？

May I have a receipt?
Wǒ néng bù néng yào zhāng shōujù?
我能不能要张收据？

May I try it (them) on?
Wǒ néng bù néng shì yíxià?
我能不能试一下？

Where do I pay?
Zài nálǐ fùkuǎn?
在哪里付款？

May I have a refund?
Wǒ néng bù néng dédào tuìkuǎn?
我能不能得到退款？

I'm just looking
Wǒ zhǐshì kànkan
我只是看看

I'll come back later
Wǒ guò yíhuìr huílái
我过一会儿回来

I'd like to buy 1kg/500g . . .
Wǒ xiǎng mǎi yì gōngjīn/yìjīn . . .
我想买一公斤／一斤...

How much does it cost per kilo?
Duōshǎo qián yì gōngjīn?
多少钱一公斤?

That's too expensive
Tài guì le
太贵了

That's enough
Gòu le
够了

Can you help me, please?
Nǐ néng bù néng bāngzhù wǒ?
你能不能帮助我?

THINGS YOU'LL SEE

百货大楼	bǎihuòdàlóu	department store
办公用品	bàngōng yòngpǐn	office supplies
部	bù	department
不退不换	bú tuì bú huàn	no exchange or refunds
副食品商店	fùshípǐn shāngdiàn	groceries
服装店	fúzhuāngdiàn	clothes store
糕点店	gāodiǎndiàn	pastry shop
工艺美术商店	gōngyì měishù shāngdiàn	arts and crafts shop
顾客止步	gùkè zhǐ bù	no entry for customers

→

价格	jiàgé	price
减价出售	jiǎnjià chūshòu	reduced price
经理办公室	jīnglǐ bàngōng shì	manager's office
咖啡厅	kāfēitīng	café
科技书店	kējì shūdiàn	science and technology bookstore
楼上	lóushàng	upper floor
楼下	lóuxià	lower floor
面包店	miànbāodiàn	bakery
男装	nánzhuāng	menswear
女装	nǚzhuāng	women's clothing
请勿用手摸	qǐng wù yòng shǒu mō	please do not touch
收款台	shōukuǎntái	cashier
书店	shūdiàn	bookstore
童装	tóngzhuāng	children's wear
外文书店	wàiwén shūdiàn	foreign language bookstore
玩具	wánjù	toys
文具店	wénjùdiàn	stationery store
闲人免进	xiánrén miǎn jìn	staff only
鞋店	xiédiàn	shoe store
烟酒店	yānjǐdiàn	tobacco and liquor store
自选商场	zìxuǎn shāngchǎng	self-service store

THINGS YOU'LL HEAR

Méiyǒu
(We) don't have any

Nǐ yào xiē shénme?
What would you like?

Wǒ néng bāng nǐ zuò xiē shénme?
Can I help you?

Nǐ yǒu méi yǒu língqián?
Do you have any change?

Duìbùqǐ, méi yǒu le
I'm sorry, we're out of stock

Hái yào biéde ma?
Will there be anything else?

Yào bú yào?
Do you want it?

POST OFFICES

Each large town has an international post office, often with English-speaking staff. International packages must be sent from these post offices. Customs officials must examine the contents of a package before it can be sent abroad, so don't seal your package before the examination. These post offices also have a poste-restante facility, and a package collection service, since packages are not delivered.

Local post offices are painted green, with green mail boxes, although airmail should be mailed in a blue mail box (if available). It is possible to buy international letter stamps at local post offices. Post offices are open seven days a week, in general from 9 AM to 6 PM. The internal postal service tends to be slow. A telegram is faster, quite inexpensive, and can be written in English if mailed from a larger, although not necessarily international, post office. Most large hotels also have a small, and often international, post office.

USEFUL WORDS AND PHRASES

airmail	hángkōng yóujiàn	航空邮件
collection	kāixiāng shíjiān	开箱时间
counter	guìtái	柜台
customs form	guānshuìbiǎo	关税表
delivery	sòngxìn	送信
domestic mail	guónèi yóujiàn	国内邮件
express telegram	jiājí diànbào	加急电报
form	biǎogé	表格
international mail	guójì yóujiàn	国际邮件
letter	xìn	信
mail (*noun*)	yóujiàn	邮件
mail (*verb*)	yóujì	邮寄

mailbox *(at home)*	xìnxiāng	信箱
mailbox	yóutǒng	邮筒
mail carrier	yóudìyuán	邮递员
package/parcel	bāoguǒ	包裹
printed matter	yìnshuāpǐn	印刷品
postage rates	yóufèi	邮费
postal/zip code	yóuzhèng biānmǎ	邮政编码
postal order	yóuzhèng huìpiào	邮政汇票
postcard	míngxìnpiàn	明信片
poste-restante	dàilǐng yóujiàn	待领邮件
post office	yóujú	邮局
registered letter	guàhàoxìn	挂号信
stamp	yóupiào	邮票
surface mail	pǔtōng yóujiàn	普通邮件
telegram	diànbào	电报

How much is a letter/postcard to . . .?
Jì wǎng . . . de xìn/míngxìnpiàn duōshǎo qián?
寄往...的信／明信片多少钱？

I would like three 20 fen stamps
Wó xiǎngyào sān zhāng liǎng jiǎo de yóupiào
我想要三张两角的邮票

I would like to register this letter
Wó xiǎng jì fēng guàhàoxìn
我想寄封挂号信

I would like to send this package to . . .
Wó xiǎng bǎ zhège bāoguǒ jì wǎng . . .
我想把这个包裹寄往...

How long does the mail to . . . take?
Jì wǎng . . . de yóujiàn yào duōcháng shíjiān?
寄往...的邮件要多长时间?

Where can I mail this?
Wǒ kéyǐ zài shénme dìfāng jì zhège?
我可以在什么地方寄这个?

Is there any mail for me?
Yóu wǒde xìn ma?
有我的信吗?

I'd like to send a telegram
Wó xiǎng pāi ge diànbào
我想拍个电报

This is to go airmail
Zhège yòng hángkōng jì
这个用航空寄

THINGS YOU'LL SEE

包裹	**bāoguǒ**	packages
待领邮件	**dàilǐng yóujiàn**	poste-restante
电报	**diànbào**	telegrams
地址	**dìzhǐ**	address
费用	**fèiyòng**	charge
挂号信	**guàhàoxìn**	registered mail
国际邮资	**guójì yóuzī**	overseas postage

→

国内邮资	guónèi yóuzī	domestic postage
海关	hǎiguān	customs
航空邮件	hángkōng yóujiàn	airmail
汇款	huìkuǎn	postal orders (dispatch)
汇票	huìpiào	postal order
寄信人	jìxìnrén	sender
开箱时间	kāi xiāng shíjiān	collection times
快递	kuàidì	express
明信片	míngxìnpiàn	postcards
请填一下表	qǐng tián yīxià biǎo	please fill in the form
取款	qúkuǎn	postal orders (collection)
收信人姓名	shōuxìnrén xìngmíng	addressee
信	xìn	letter
信箱	xìnxiāng	mailbox (at home)
营业时间	yíngyè shíjiān	opening hours
邮件	yóujiàn	mail
邮局	yóujú	post office
邮票	yóupiào	stamps
邮筒	yóutǒng	mailbox
邮政编码	yóuzhèng biānmǎ	postal code/zip code
邮资	yóuzī	postage

BANKS AND MONEY

Traveler's checks and foreign currency can be exchanged at hotel banks or at the Bank of China, which has branches in all tourist cities and employs English-speaking staff.

The foreign exchange counters in banks are usually open Monday to Friday, from 9 AM to noon and 2–5 PM. The Chinese unit of currency is the *"yuán,"* which is broken down into ten *"jiǎo"* and one hundred *"fēn."* In spoken Mandarin, *"yuán"* is usually referred to as *"kuài,"* and *"jiǎo"* as *"máo."* Currency is issued in 1, 2, and 5 *"fēn"* notes and coins; 1, 2, and 5 *"jiǎo"* notes; and 1, 2, 5, 10, 50, and 100 *"yuán"* notes.

Credit cards can be used in China, although only in a few places. Large hotels, friendship stores, large CITS offices, important restaurants, and banks will generally accept most main cards, but outside major cities, only banks will take them.

USEFUL WORDS AND PHRASES

bank	yínháng	银行
bill *(currency)*	chāopiào	钞票
change *(verb)*	duìhuàn	兑换
check	zhīpiào	支票
deposit	chǔxù	储蓄
exchange rate	huìlǜ	汇率
foreign exchange	wàihuì duìhuàn	外汇兑换
international money order	guójì huìpiào	国际汇票
Japanese yen	rìyuán	日元
money order	huìpiào	汇票
pound sterling	yīngbàng	英镑
traveler's cheque	lǚxíng zhīpiào	旅行支票
US dollar	měiyuán	美元

I'd like to change this into . . .
Wó xiǎng bǎ zhège huànchéng . . .
我想把这个换成...

Can I cash these traveler's checks?
Wǒ néng bù néng bǎ zhèxie lǔxín zhìpiào duìhuàncheng
   xiànkuǎn?
我能不能把这些旅行支票兑换成现款?

What is the exchange rate for the US dollar?
Měiyuán de huìlǜ shì duōshǎo?
美元的汇率是多少?

Can I draw cash using this credit card?
Wǒ néng yòng zhèzhāng xìnyòng kǎ qǔ qián ma?
我能用这张信用卡取钱吗?

THINGS YOU'LL HEAR

Qíng chūshì hùzhào
May I see your passport, please?

Qíng tiánxiě cǐ biǎoge
Fill in this form

TELEPHONES

The phone system in China is expanding rapidly. International calls can often be made directly, depending on where you are calling to and from. Generally, calls are made through the international operator, who usually speaks English. You can phone either by booking a call through your hotel's operator, or by going to the Post and Telecommunications main office (*yóu diàn dà lóu*) in the town you are in and booking a call at the international counter, then waiting for a connection. You will also see staffed public telephone spots on the streets, from which you can make direct international and internal calls without booking. A small fee will be added to the cost of the call.

Internal calls can be made from Post and Telecommunications offices or from public phone booths. There are card phones in cities, which can be used for long-distance calls, while other public telephone booths are usually only for local calls. The internal phone system can be inefficient in small towns and remote areas, often meaning delays or a bad connection.

From most hotels and work units local calls are free, but not from public phones. Internal call rates depend on the distance called.

USEFUL WORDS AND PHRASES

busy	zhànxiàn	占线
call (*noun*)	diànhuà	电话
call (*verb*)	dǎ diànhuà	打电话
code	dìqū hàomǎ	地区号码
collect call	duìfāng fùkuǎn	对方付款
dial (*verb*)	bōhào	拨号
dial tone	bōhào xìnhào	拨号信号
directory inquiries	cháhàotái	查号台
extension	(diànhuà) fēnjī	（电话）分机

external phone	wàixiàn diànhuà	外线电话
internal phone	nèixiàn diànhuà	内线电话
international call	guójì chángtú	国际长途
number	diànhuà hàomǎ	电话号码
operator	jiēxiànyuán	接线员
pay phone	jìfèi diànhuà	计费电话
public phone	gōngyòng diànhuà	公用电话
telephone	diànhuà	电话
telephone booth	diànhuàtíng	电话亭
telephone directory	diànhuà hàomǎ bù	电话号码薄
wrong number	hàomǎ cuòle	号码错了

Where is the nearest phone booth?
Zuì jìn de diànhuàtíng zài nálǐ?
最近的电话亭在哪里？

Can you tell me the number for . . .?
Néng bù néng gàosù wǒ . . . de diànhuà hàomǎ?
能不能告诉我...的电话号码？

Can I call abroad from here?
Zhèli néng bù néng guà guójì chángtú?
这里能不能挂国际长途？

I would like to make a collect call
Wǒ xiǎng jiào duìfāng fùkuǎn
我想叫对方付款

How long will I have to wait for a connection?
Yào duōcháng shíjiān néng jiētōng?
要多长时间能接通？

Hello, this is . . . speaking
Wèi, wǒ shì . . .
喂，我是...

Is that . . .?
Nǐ shì . . . ma?
你是...吗?

Please speak slowly
Qǐng shuō màn yíxiē
请说慢一些

Speaking
Wǒ jiù shì
我就是

I would like to speak to . . .
Wó xiáng zhǎo . . . jiē diànhuà
我想找...接电话

Please tell him . . . called
Qǐng zhuǎngào tā, . . . gěi tā dǎ diànhuà le
请转告他，...给他打电话了

Could you ask her to call me back, please
Qǐng ràng tā géi wǒ huíge diànhuà
请让她给我回个电话

My number is . . .
Wǒde diànhuà hàomǎ shì . . .
我的电话号码是...

Do you know where he is?
Nǐ zhīdào tā zài nálǐ ma?
你知道他在哪里吗？

When will he be back?
Tā shénme shíhòu huílái?
他什么时候回来？

Could you leave him a message?
Néng bù néng gěi tā liú ge tiáozi?
能不能给他留个条子？

I'll call back later
Wǒ guò yíhuir zài dǎ
我过一会儿再打

Sorry, wrong number
Duìbùqǐ, hàomǎ cuòle
对不起，号码错了

I can't hear you
Wǒ tīng bù qīng
我听不清

THINGS YOU'LL SEE

长途电话	chángtú diànhuà	long-distance calls
电话	diànhuà	telephone
电话亭	diànhuàtíng	telephone booth
地区号	dìqūhào	code
公用电话	gōngyòng diànhuà	public phone
国际电话	guójì diànhuà	international calls
坏了	huàile	out of order ⟶

郊区电话	**jiāoqū diànhuà**	local/district calls
接线员	**jiēxiànyuán**	operator
市内电话	**shìnèi diànhuà**	local calls (inside city)
收费	**shōufèi**	charges
直拨电话	**zhíbō diànhuà**	direct dialing

REPLIES YOU MAY BE GIVEN

Nǐ zhǎo shuí?
Who would you like to speak to?

Shì nǐ fùkuǎn ma?
Are you paying for the call yourself?

Shì duìfāng fùkuǎn ma?
Is this a collect call?

Nǐ bǎ hàomǎ gǎo cuò le
You've got the wrong number

Nǐ dǎ shénme hàomǎ?
What number are you calling?

Nǐ shì shuí ya?
Who's speaking?

Wèi
Hello

Nǐde diànhuà hàomǎ shì duōshǎo?
What is your number?

→

Duìbuqǐ, tā bú zài
Sorry, he's/she's not in

Tā ... diǎnzhōng huílái
He'll/she'll be back at . . . o'clock

Qǐng nǐ míngtiān zài dǎ lái ba
Please call again tomorrow

Wǒ huì gàosù tā nǐ láiguò diànhuà le
I'll tell him/her you called

HEALTH

The standard of health care in China varies dramatically depending on who you are and where you are, but be prepared for rather basic conditions, if comparing to Western standards.

Most hotels have a doctor to whom guests are referred and it is advisable to see this doctor first. If you continue to feel ill, ask for advice on which hospital to go to. If you think you may be seriously ill, try to insist on being admitted to the cadre (gànbù) section of a good hospital, since conditions there are generally much better.

Before seeing a doctor, you must report to the hospital registration desk, where you will pay a small fee and receive a booklet to give to the doctor. In most Chinese hospitals, there is no appointment system—it's a matter of joining the relevant line. Consultations are rarely in private, but it is possible to close the door yourself, if it would make things easier for you.

Once admitted to a hospital, it is common practice to link the patient to an IV drip, usually glucose. Drips and injections are used a lot in Chinese hospitals, which can be quite upsetting for a foreigner. Often there will be no meals, so you may have to arrange for friends to bring food to you. Chinese doctors often avoid telling the patient exactly what is wrong, particularly if the illness is serious, but he or she will usually discuss the case a little more openly with a friend of the patient. If necessary, the hospital will be able to find an interpreter for you.

Medicine can be bought in a hospital with a prescription, or from a pharmacist with or without a prescription. Hospital treatment involving a stay in a hospital varies in cost, and the precise amount is often hard to establish until the bill is presented. Both treatment and medicine are, however, usually less expensive than in Western countries.

Doctors may ask if you would prefer Western or Chinese medicine and treatment. On the whole, Chinese medicine uses natural products. Most towns have Chinese medicine hospitals, and these usually welcome foreign patients. Prescriptions can only be collected from a Chinese medicine pharmacist.

USEFUL WORDS AND PHRASES

abscess	nóngzhǒng	脓肿
accident	shìgù	事故
acupuncture	zhēnjiǔ	针灸
ambulance	jiùhùchē	救护车
appendicitis	lánwěiyán	阑尾炎
aspirin	āsīpǐlín	阿斯匹林
asthma	xiāochuǎn	哮喘
backache	bèiténg	背疼
bandage	bēngdài	绷带
bandage (*adhesive*)	gāo yào	膏药
bite	yǎoshāng	咬伤
blood	xuè	血
blood pressure	xuèyā	血压
burn	shāoshāng	烧伤
cancer	ái	癌
chest	xiōngqiāng	胸腔
chicken pox	shuǐdòu	水痘
Chinese medicine	zhōngyào	中药
cold (*noun*)	gǎnmào	感冒
concussion	nǎozhèndàng	脑震荡
constipation	biànbì	便秘
cough	késòu	咳嗽
cut	dāoshāng	刀伤
dentist	yákē yīshēng	牙科医生
diarrhea	lā dùzi	拉肚子

doctor	yīshēng	医生
earache	ěrduōténg	耳朵疼
fever	fāshāo	发烧
filling	bǔyá	补牙
first aid	jíjiù	急救
flu	liúxíngxìng gǎnmào	流行性感冒
fracture	gǔzhé	骨折
hay fever	huāfěnrè	花粉热
headache	tóuténg	头疼
heart	xīnzàng	心脏
heart attack	xīnzàngbìng	心脏病
hemorrhage	nèi chūxuè	内出血
hepatitis	gānyán	肝炎
hospital	yīyuàn	医院
ill	shēngbìng	生病
indigestion	xiāohuà bù liáng	消化不良
injection	dǎzhēn	打针
itch	yǎng	痒
kidney	shènzàng	肾脏
lump	zhǒngkuài	肿块
measles	mázhěn	麻疹
migraine	piāntóutòng	偏头痛
motion sickness	yūnchē	晕车
mumps	liúxíngxìng sāixiànyán	流行性腮腺炎
nausea	ěxīn	恶心
nurse	hùshì	护士

operation	shǒushù	手术
optician	yǎnkē yīshēng	眼科医生
pain	téng	疼
penicillin	pánníxīlín	盘尼西林
pharmacist	yàofáng	药房
plaster of Paris	shóushígāo	熟石膏
pneumonia	fèiyán	肺炎
pregnant	huáiyùn	怀孕
prescription	yàofāng	药方
rheumatism	fēngshībìng	风湿病
septic	huànóng	化脓
sore	téng	疼
sore throat	sǎngziténg	嗓子疼
sprain	niǔshāng	扭伤
sting	cìtòng	刺痛
stomach	wèi	胃
temperature	tǐwēn	体温
tonsils	biǎntáoxiàn	扁桃腺
toothache	yáténg	牙疼
ulcer	kuíyáng	溃疡
vaccination	yùfáng jīezhǒng	预防接种
vomit (*verb*)	ǒutù	呕吐
Western medicine	xīyào	西药
X-ray	"X" guāng	"爱克斯" 光

I have a pain in . . .
Wǒ . . . téng
我...疼

I don't feel well
Wó gǎnjué bù shūfú
我感觉不舒服

I feel sick
Wó gǎndào ěxīn
我感到恶心

I feel dizzy
Wǒ tóuyūn
我头晕

I would like to go the cadres' wing
Wó xiǎng qù gāogàn bìngfáng
我想去高干病房

I don't want an IV drip
Wǒ bù xiǎngyào shūyè
我不想要输液

It hurts here
Zhèli téng
这里疼

How do I take the medicine?
Zhège yào zěnme fúfǎ?
这个药怎么服法?

It's a sharp pain
Téng de lìhài
疼得厉害

It's a dull pain
Yǐnyin de téng
隐隐的疼

It hurts all the time
Yìzhí téng
一直疼

It only hurts now and then
Yǒude shíhòu téng
有的时候疼

It hurts when you touch it
Pèng shí téng
碰时疼

It hurts more at night
Wǎnshàng téng de gèng lìhài
晚上疼得更厉害

It stings
Xiàng zhēnzhā yíyàng téng
象针扎一样疼

It aches
Suānténg
酸疼

I have a temperature
Wǒ fāshāole
我发烧了

I need a prescription for . . .
Wǒ xūyào kāi yíge zhì . . . de yàofāng
我需要开一个治...的药方

Please explain what is wrong with me
Qǐng gàosù wǒ shì shénme máobìng
请告诉我是什么毛病

I normally take . . .
Wǒ tōngcháng yòng . . .
我通常用...

Where can I get something to eat?
Nálǐ yǒu chī de?
哪里有吃的?

Where can I take a shower?
Línyù zài nálǐ?
淋浴在哪里?

When can I take a shower?
Shénme shíjiān kéyǐ línyù?
什么时间可以淋浴?

I'm allergic to . . .
Wǒ duì . . . guòmǐn
我对...过敏

Have you got anything for . . .?
Ní yǒu zhì . . . de yào ma?
你有治...的药吗?

I have lost a filling
Wǒde yá bǔguò yòu diào le
我的牙补过又掉了

Where can I buy this medicine?
Nálǐ néng mǎidào zhège yào?
哪里能买到这个药?

Can I pay for the medicine here?
Wǒ kéyǐ zài zhèli fù yàoqián ma?
我可以在这里付药钱吗?

I want to register to see the doctor
Wó xiǎng guà ge hào
我想挂个号

Can I see an English-speaking doctor?
Wǒ néng bù néng zhǎoge huì shuō Yīngyǔ de yīshēng?
我能不能找个会说英语的医生?

THINGS YOU'LL SEE

儿科	**érkē**	pediatrics
妇科	**fùkē**	gynecology
挂号处	**guàhàochù**	registration desk
骨科	**gǔkē**	orthopedics
救护车	**jiùhùchē**	ambulance
内科	**nèikē**	medical
取药处	**qǔyàochù**	prescription collection office
外科	**wàikē**	surgery
五官科	**wǔguānkē**	ear, nose, and throat specialist
"爱克斯" 光	**"X" guāng**	X-ray
医务所	**yīwùsuǒ**	clinic
医院	**yīyuàn**	hospital
值班药剂师	**zhíbān yàojìshī**	pharmacist on duty

→

99

| 中医科 | zhōngyīkē | Chinese medicine department |
| 专家门诊 | zhuānjiā ménzhěn | specialist clinic (Chinese medicine) |

THINGS YOU'LL HEAR

Nǐ nálǐ bù shūfú?
What seems to be the problem?

Nǐ guàhào le ma?
Have you registered at the front desk?

MINI-DICTIONARY

a yígè — 一个

accident shìgù — 事故

adaptor (*plug*) duōyòng chātóu — 多用插头

address dìzhǐ — 地址

after yǐhòu — 以后

again zài — 再

air conditioning kōngtiáo — 空调

airport fēijīchǎng — 飞机场

alarm clock nàozhōng — 闹钟

alcohol jiǔjīng — 酒精

all suóyǒu — 所有

  all the streets suóyǒu de jiēdào — 所有的街道

  that's all, thanks hǎole, xièxie — 好了，谢谢

almost chàbuduō — 差不多

alone dāndú — 单独

already yǐjīng — 已经

also yě — 也

always zǒngshì — 总是

America Měiguó — 美国

American (*adj.*) Měiguó — 美国

and hé — 和

another (*different*) lìng yígè — 另一个

  (*further*) yòu yígè — 又一个

antibiotics kàngjūnsù — 抗菌素

antiseptic fángfǔjì — 防腐剂

apartment dānyuán — 单元

apple píngguǒ	苹果
appointment book rìjì	日记
arm gēbo	胳膊
arrive dàodá	到达
art yìshù	艺术
ashtray yānhuīgāng	烟灰缸
asleep: he's asleep tā shuìzháo le	他睡着了
at zài	在
at the café zài kāfēi guǎn	在咖啡馆
attractive mírénde	迷人的
aunt (*maternal*) yímā	姨妈
(*paternal*) gūmā	姑妈
Australia Àodàlìyà	澳大利亚
Australian (*adj.*) Àodàlìyà	澳大利亚
awful zāotòule	糟透了
baby yīng'ér	婴儿
back (*body*) bèi	背
backpack bèibāo	背包
back street hòujiē	后街
bad huài	坏
baggage xínglǐ	行李
baggage storage xínglǐ jìcúnchù	行李寄存处
ball qiú	球
bamboo zhúzi	竹子
bamboo shoots zhúsǔn	竹笋
banana xiāngjiāo	香蕉
band (*music*) yuèduì	乐队
bandage bēngdài	绷带

bank yínháng   银行

bar jiǔbā   酒吧

barber lǐfàshī   理发师

bath xǐzǎo   洗澡

bathing suit yóuyǒngyī   游泳衣

bathroom xǐzǎojiān   洗澡间

battery diànchí   电池

beach hǎitān   海滩

beans dòu   豆

beard húzi   胡子

beautiful (*in appearance*) piāoliàng   漂亮

because yīnwèi   因为

bed chuáng   床

bedroom wòshì   卧室

beef niúròu   牛肉

beer píjiǔ   啤酒

before zài . . . yǐqián   在...以前

begin kāishǐ   开始

behind zài . . . hòumiàn   在...后面

bell zhōng   钟

  (*for door, school*) líng   铃

below zài . . . xiàmiàn   在...下面

belt (*clothing*) yāodài   腰带

best: the best zuìhǎo   最好

better gèng hǎo   更好

between zài . . . zhījiān   在...之间

bicycle zìxíngchē   自行车

big dà   大

bikini bǐjīní   比基尼

bill zhàngdān		帐单
birthday shēngrì		生日
happy birthday! shēngrì kuàilè!		生日快乐！
bitter *(taste)* kǔ		苦
black hēi		黑
blanket tǎnzi		毯子
blind xiā		瞎
blinds bǎiyè chuāng		百叶窗
blocked *(road, drain)* dǔzhùle		堵住了
blond *(adj.)* jīnhuángsè		金黄色
blouse nǔchènshān		女衬衫
blue lánsè		蓝色
boat chuán		船
body shēntǐ		身体
boiled rice mǐfàn		米饭
book *(noun)* shū		书
bookstore shūdiàn		书店
boot xuēzi		靴子
border *(of country)* biānjiè		边界
boring méi jìng		没劲
boss láobǎn		老板
both liǎngge dāu		两个都
bottle píngzi		瓶子
bottle opener píng gài kāi dāo		瓶盖开刀
bowl wǎn		碗
box hézi		盒子
boxer quánjīshǒu		拳击手
boy nánhái		男孩
boyfriend nán péngyou		男朋友

bra xiōngzhào	胸罩
bracelet shǒuzhuó	手镯
brandy báilándì	白兰地
bread miànbāo	面包
breakfast zǎofàn	早饭
bridge *(over river, etc.)* qiáo	桥
briefcase gōngwénbāo	公文包
Britain Yīngguó	英国
British *(adj.)* Yīngguó	英国
broken *(out of order)* huàile	坏了
(leg) duànle	断了
brooch xiōngzhēn	胸针
brother xiōngdì	兄弟
brown zōngsè	棕色
bruise shānghén	伤痕
brush shuāzi	刷子
Buddha Fó	佛
building fángzi	房子
bulb *(light)* dēng pào	灯泡
bungalow píngfáng	平房
burglar qièzéi	窃贼
Burma Miǎndiàn	缅甸
burn *(noun)* shāoshāng	烧伤
bus gōnggòng qìchē	公共汽车
business shēngyì	生意
businessman shāngrén	商人
bus station gōnggòng qìchē zǒng zhàn	公共汽车总站
bus stop chēzhàn	车站

busy (*street*) rènào 热闹
  (*restaurant*) hěn máng 很忙
but dànshì 但是
butter huángyóu 黄油
button niǔkòu 纽扣
buy mǎi 买
by yóu 由
  by train/car zuò huǒchē/xiǎo qìchē 坐火车 / 小汽车

café kāfēiguǎn 咖啡馆
cake dàngāo 蛋糕
calculator jìsuànqì 计算器
call: what is this called? 这叫什么？
  zhè jiào shénme?
camera zhàoxiàngjī 照相机
can (*tin*) guàntou 罐头
can: can I . . .? wǒ kěyǐ . . . ma? 我可以...吗？
  can you . . .? nǐ néng bù néng . . .? 你能不能...？
  he can't . . . tā bù néng . . . 他不能...
Canada Jiānádà 加拿大
candy táng 糖
can opener guàntou qǐzi 罐头起子
Cantonese (*adj.*) Guǎngdōng 广东
  (*language*) Guǎngdōnghuà 广东话
cap màozi 帽子
car xiǎo qìchē 小汽车
card (*business*) míngpiàn 名片
careful: be careful! xiǎoxīn! 小心！
carpet dìtǎn 地毯
106

cash (*money*) xiànjīn 现金

cassette cídài 磁带

center (*of town*) zhōngxīn 中心

chair yǐzi 椅子

change (*noun: money*) língqián 零钱

  (*verb: money*) duì huàn 兑换

  (*verb: clothes, trains*) huàn 换

check zhīpiào 支票

check book zhīpiàoběn 支票本

check cashing card zhīpiàokǎ 支票卡

cheers! (*toast*) gānbēi 干杯！

cheese nǎilào 奶酪

chef chúshī 厨师

chess xiàngqí 象棋

chest (*body*) xiōngkǒu 胸口

chewing gum kǒuxiāngtáng 口香糖

chicken jī 鸡

  (*meat*) jīròu 鸡肉

child, children háizi 孩子

chili pepper làjiāofěn 辣椒粉

China Zhōngguó 中国

China tea Zhōngguo chá 中国茶

Chinese (*adj.*) Zhōngguo 中国

  (*person*) Zhōngguoren 中国人

  (*language*) Hànyǔ 汉语

  the Chinese Zhōngguó rénmín 中国人民

Chinese-style Zhōngshì 中式

chocolate qiǎokelì 巧克力

chopsticks kuàizi 筷子

church jiàotáng	教堂
cigar xuějiā	雪茄
cigarette xiāng yān	香烟
city chéngshì	城市
clean *(adj.)* gānjìng	干净
clever cōngming	聪明
clock zhōng	钟
close: to be close *(near)* jìn	近
closed guānle	关了
clothes yīfu	衣服
clothes pin yīfu jiāzi	衣服夹子
coast hǎibīn	海滨
coat *(overcoat)* dàyī	大衣
(jacket) wàiyī	外衣
coat hanger yījià	衣架
cockroach zhāngláng	蟑螂
coconut yēzi	椰子
coconut milk yēzi zhī	椰子汁
coffee kāfēi	咖啡
cold lěng	冷
I have a cold wó gǎnmàole	我感冒了
collect call duìfāng fùkuǎn	对方付款
color yánsè	颜色
comb shūzi	梳子
come lái	来
I come from . . . wǒ lái zì . . .	我来自...
come in! qǐng jìn	请进
Communist Party gòngchǎndǎng	共产党

Communist Party member　　　　共产党员
　gòngchándǎngyuán

company *(firm)* gōngsī　　　　　公司

complicated fùzá　　　　　　　　复杂

computer jìsuànjī　　　　　　　　计算机

concert yīnyuèhuì　　　　　　　　音乐会

condom bìyùntào　　　　　　　　避孕套

consulate lǐngshìguǎn　　　　　　领事馆

contact lenses yǐnxíng yǎnjìng　　隐形眼镜

cookie bǐnggān　　　　　　　　　饼干

cool *(day, weather)* liángkuai　　　凉快

corner: on the corner guáijiǎo chù　拐角处

　in the corner zài jiǎoluò lǐ　　　　在角落里

cost jià qián　　　　　　　　　　价钱

　what does it cost? zhè yào　　　这要多少钱?
　duōshǎo qián?

cot diào chuáng/yīng'ér chuáng　　吊床 / 婴儿床

cotton miánhuā　　　　　　　　　棉花

cotton balls yàomián　　　　　　　药棉

cough *(verb)* késou　　　　　　　咳嗽

country *(nation)* guójiā　　　　　国家

crab pángxiè　　　　　　　　　　螃蟹

cramp jìngluán　　　　　　　　　痉挛

cream *(to eat)* nǎiyóu　　　　　　奶油

credit card xìnyòng kǎ　　　　　　信用卡

crocodile èyú　　　　　　　　　　鳄鱼

crowd rénqún　　　　　　　　　　人群

Cultural Revolution　　　　　　　文化大革命
　Wénhuà Dàgémìng

cup bēizi	杯子
a cup of coffee yī bēi kāfēi	一杯咖啡
curry gālí	咖喱
curtains chuānglián	窗帘
Customs hǎiguān	海关
cut qiè	切
cyclist qí zìxíngchē de rén	骑自行车的人
dangerous wēixiǎn	危险
dark hēi àn	黑暗
daughter nǚ'ér	女儿
day bái tiān	白天
dead sǐle	死了
deaf ěr lóng	耳聋
deep shēn	深
delicious hǎochī	好吃
dentist yákē yīshēng	牙科医生
deodorant chúchòujì	除臭剂
departure chūfā	出发
develop (film) chōngxǐ	冲洗
dictionary zìdiǎn	字典
die sǐ	死
different bùtóng	不同
difficult kùnnan	困难
dinner wǎnfàn	晚饭
dirty zāng	脏
disabled cánfèi	残废
disco dísīkē	迪斯科
divorced líhūnle	离婚了

do zuò   做

doctor yīsheng   医生

dog gǒu   狗

dollar měiyuán   美元

don't! búyào!   不要！

door mén   门

down: down there xiàmiàn nàlǐ   下面那里

dress (*woman's*) liányīqún   连衣裙

drink (*verb*) hē   喝

drinking water yǐnyòngshuǐ   饮用水

driver's license jiàshǐ zhízhào   驾驶执照

drunk zuì   醉

dry gān   干

dry cleaner's gānxǐdiàn   干洗店

dynasty cháo dài   朝代

  the Ming/Ch'ing Dynasty   明朝／清朝
  Míngcháo/Qīngcháo

each měi yíge   每一个

ear ěrduo   耳朵

early zǎo   早

earring ěrhuán   耳环

east dōng   东

easy róngyì   容易

eat chī   吃

egg jīdàn   鸡蛋

egg noodles jīdàn miàn   鸡蛋面

either . . . or . . . bú shì . . . jiùshi . . . 不是...就是...

elastic yǒu tánxìng de   有弹性的

electricity diàn	电
elevator *(in hotel, etc.)* diàntī	电梯
else: something else biéde dōngxi	别的东西
somewhere else biéde dìfāng	别的地方
embarrassing gāngà	尴尬
embassy dàshíguǎn	大使馆
emergency jǐnjí qíngkuàng	紧急情况
emperor huángdì	黄帝
empty kōng	空
end *(noun)* mòduān	末端
engaged *(to be married)* dìnghūnle	订婚了
England Yīnggélán	英格兰
English *(adj.)* Yīnggélán	英格兰
(language) Yīngyǔ	英语
enough gòule	够了
entrance rùkǒu	入口
envelope xìnfēng	信封
eraser xiàngpí	橡皮
evening wǎnshàng	晚上
every měiyíge	每一个
everyone měiyíge rén	每一个人
everything měijiàn shìqíng	每件事情
everywhere měige dìfāng	每个地方
excellent hǎojíle	好极了
excuse me *(to get attention)* láo jià	劳驾
(pardon?) qǐng zài shuō yíbiàn, hǎo ma?	请再说一遍，好吗?
exit chūkǒu	出口
expensive guì	贵
eye yǎnjīng	眼睛

face liǎn	脸
factory gōngchǎng	工厂
family jiātíng	家庭
fan (*mechanical*) fēngshàn	风扇
(*hand-held*) shànzi	扇子
far (*away*) yuǎn	远
farmer nóngmín	农民
fashion liúxíng shìyàng	流行式样
fast kuài	快
fat (*person*) pàng	胖
father bàba	爸爸
feel gǎnjué	感觉
I feel hot wǒ juéde rè	我觉得热
ferry dùchuán	渡船
fever fāshāo	发烧
few: a few yìxiē	一些
fiancé(e) wèi hūn fū/qī	未婚夫 / 妻
field tiándì	田地
(*rice, paddy*) dàotián	稻田
film (*camera*) jiāojuǎn	胶卷
(*movie*) diànyǐng	电影
find zhǎo	找
finger shǒu zhítou	手指头
fire huǒ	火
there's a fire! zháohuǒ la!	著火啦！
fire extinguisher mièhuǒqì	灭火器
first dìyī	第一
fish yú	鱼
fisherman yúmín	渔民

fishing diàoyú	钓鱼
fishing boat yúchuán	渔船
fizzy yǒuqìde	有汽的
flash (*for camera*) shǎnguāngdēng	闪光灯
flat (*adj.*) píngtǎn	平坦
flat tire chuānkǒng	穿孔
flavor wèidao	味道
flea tiàozǎo	跳蚤
flight hángbān	航班
floor (*of room*) dìbǎn	地板
(*story*) lóu	楼
flower huā	花
fly (*insect*) cāngying	苍蝇
fly (*verb*) fēi	飞
folk music mínjiān yīnyuè	民间音乐
food shíwù	食物
food poisoning shíwù zhòngdú	食物中毒
foot jiǎo	脚
for: for her wèi tā	为她
that's for me zhè shì géi wǒde	这是给我的
a bus for . . . qù . . . de gōnggòng qìchē	去...的公共汽车
forbidden jìnzhǐ	禁止
Forbidden City Zǐjìnchéng	紫禁城
foreigner wàiguoren	外国人
forest sēnlín	森林
free zìyóu	自由
(*of charge*) miǎnfèi	免费
freezer bīngguì	冰柜

French fries zhá tǔdòutiáo	炸土豆条
fried noodles chǎomiàn	炒面
fried rice chǎofàn	炒饭
friend péngyǒu	朋友
friendly yóuhǎo	友好
friendship store yǒuyí shāngdiàn	友谊商店
from: from Beijing to Shanghai	从北京到上海
cóng Běijīng dào Shànghǎi	
front qiánmiàn	前面
fruit shuíguǒ	水果
fruit juice guǒzhī	果汁
fry *(deep fry)* zhá	炸
(stir fry) chǎo	炒
full mǎn	满
I'm full wó bǎole	我饱了
funny *(strange)* qíguài	奇怪
(amusing) yǒu yìsi	有意思
garbage lājī	垃圾
garden huāyuán	花园
garlic dàsuàn	大蒜
gas qìyóu	汽油
gas station jiāyóuzhàn	加油站
gay *(homosexual)* gǎo	搞同性恋的
tóngxìngliàn de	
get *(obtain)* dé dào	得到
(fetch) qǔ	取
(train, bus, etc.) zuòchē	坐车
have you got . . . ? ní yǒu . . . ma?	你有...吗?

get in *(to car)* shàngchē   上车
  (arrive) dàodá   到达
get up *(in morning)* qǐchuáng   起床
ginger shēngjiāng   生姜
girl nǚhái   女孩
girlfriend nǚpéngyǒu   女朋友
give gěi   给
glad gāoxìng   高兴
glass *(for drinking)* bōlibēi   玻璃杯
  (material) bōli   玻璃
glasses *(spectacles)* yǎnjìng   眼镜
glue jiāoshuǐ   胶水
go qù   去
Gobi Desert Gēbìtān   戈壁滩
gold huángjīn   黄金
good hǎo   好
good-bye zàijiàn   再见
government zhèngfǔ   政府
granddaughter
  (son's daughter) sūnnǚ   孙女
  (daughter's daughter) waisūnnǚ   外孙女
grandfather *(maternal)* wàigōng   外公
  (paternal) yéye   爷爷
grandmother *(maternal)* wàipó   外婆
  (paternal) nǎinai   奶奶
grandson *(son's son)* sūnzi   孙子
  (daughter's son) wài sūnzi   外孙子
grapes pútao   葡萄
grass cǎo   草

gray huīsè   灰色

great: that's great! hǎojíle   好极了！

Great Britain Dàbùlièdiān   大不列颠

green lǜsè   绿色

green Chinese onion dàcōng   大葱

ground floor yī lóu   一楼

guide dǎoyóu   导游

guidebook dǎoyóu shǒucè   导游手册

gun *(pistol)* shǒuqiāng   手枪

   (rifle) qiāng   枪

hair tóufa   头发

haircut lǐfà   理发

hairdresser lǐfàshī   理发师

hair dryer diànchuīfēng   电吹风

half yíbàn   一半

ham huótuǐ   火腿

hamburger hànbǎobāo   汉堡包

hammer chuízi   锤子

hand shǒu   手

handbag shǒutíbāo   手提包

handkerchief shǒujuàn   手绢

handle *(noun)* báshǒu   把手

handsome yīngjùn   英俊

happy kuàilè   快乐

harbor gángkǒu   港口

hard *(material)* yìng   硬

   (difficult) nán   难

hat màozi   帽子

have yǒu   有

   do you have . . .? ní yǒu . . . ma?   你有...吗?

   I don't have . . . wǒ méiyǒu . . .   我没有...

hay fever huāfěnrè   花粉热

he tā   他

head tóu   头

headache tóuténg   头疼

headlights chētóudēng   车头灯

hear tīngjiàn   听见

hearing aid zhùtīngqì   助听器

heart xīnzàng   心脏

heat rè   热

heavy zhòng   重

heel *(shoe)* xiégēn   鞋跟

   (foot) jiǎogēn   脚跟

hello ní hǎo   你好

help *(verb)* bāngzhù   帮助

help! jiùmìng!   救命！

her *(possessive)* tāde   她的

   (object) tā   她

herbs *(cooking)* zuǒliào   佐料

   (medicine) cǎoyào   草药

here zhèlǐ   这里

hers tāde   她的

hi! ní hǎo!   你好！

high gāo   高

hill xiǎoshān   小山

him tā   他

his tāde   他的

holiday (*public*) jiérì	节日
Hong Kong Xiānggǎng	香港
horrible kěpà	可怕
hot rè	热
(*to taste*) là	辣
hotel (*superior, for foreigners*) fàndiàn	饭店
(*small*) lǚguǎn	旅馆
house fángzi	房子
how? zěnme?	怎么?
hungry: I'm hungry wǒ èle	我饿了
hurry: I'm in a hurry wǒ méi shíjiān	我没时间
husband zhàngfu	丈夫
I wǒ	我
ice bīng	冰
ice cream bīngqílín	冰淇淋
if rúguǒ	如果
ill shēng bìngle	生病了
immediately mǎshàng	马上
impossible bù kěnéng	不可能
in zài	在
in English yòng Yīngyǔ	用英语
India Yìndù	印度
inexpensive piányi	便宜
infection gǎnrǎn	感染
information xìnxī	信息
insect repellent qūchóngjì	驱虫剂
insurance bǎoxiǎn	保险
interesting yǒu yìsi	有意思

interpret zuò fānyì   做翻译

Ireland Ài'ěrlán   爱尔兰

iron *(for clothes)* yùndǒu   熨斗

island dǎo   岛

it tā   它

  it's expensive guì   贵

jack *(for car)* qiānjīndǐng   千斤顶

jacket wàitào   外套

jade yù   玉

Japan Rìběn   日本

jasmine tea mòlì huā chá   茉莉花茶

jeans niúzǎikù   牛仔裤

jewelry shǒushì   首饰

job gōngzuò   工作

jug guàn   罐

junk *(boat)* fānchuán   帆船

just *(only)* jǐnjin   仅仅

  just one jiù yīge   就一个

key yàoshi   钥匙

kilo gōngjīn   公斤

kilometer gōnglǐ   公里

kitchen chúfáng   厨房

knee xīgài   膝盖

knife dāo   刀

know: I don't know wǒ bù zhīdào   我不知道

Korea: North Korea Běi Cháoxiǎn   北朝鲜

  South Korea Nán Cháoxiǎn   南朝鲜

lady nǚshì	女士
lake hú	湖
lane xiǎoxiàng	小巷
Laos Lǎowō	老挝
large dà	大
last *(previous)* shàng yíge	上一个
(final) zuìhòu	最后
last year qùnián	去年
late *(at night)* wǎn	晚
(behind schedule) chí	迟
later yǐhòu	以后
laundry detergent xǐyīfěn	洗衣粉
left *(not right)* zuǒ	左
leg tuǐ	腿
lemon níngméng	柠檬
lemonade níngméng qìshuǐ	柠檬汽水
letter *(in mail)* xìn	信
lettuce wōju	莴苣
library túshūguǎn	图书馆
life shēnghuó	生活
lift: could you give me a lift? nǐ néng bù néng ràng wǒ dāge chē?	你能不能让我搭个车？
light *(noun)* dēng	灯
have you got a light? jiè ge huǒ, xíng ma?	借个火，行吗？
(not heavy) qīng	轻
light bulb dēngpào	灯泡
lighter dáhuǒjī	打火机
like: I would like a . . . wó xiǎng . . .	我想…

I like you wó xǐhuān nǐ   我喜欢你

  one like that xiàng nèige yíyàng   象那个一样

line (*of people*) duì   队

lipstick kǒuhóng   口红

liter shēng   升

little xiǎo   小

  just a little jiù yìdiǎndian   就一点点

liver gān   肝

lobster lóngxiā   龙虾

long cháng   长

  how long does it take?   要多长时间?
  yào duōcháng shíjiān?

lose: I've lost my . . . wǒ . . . diūle   我...丢了

lost and found   失物招领处
  shīwù zhāolǐng chù

lot: a lot xǔduō   许多

  a lot of money xǔ duō qián   许多钱

loud dàshēng de   大声的

love: I love you wǒ ài nǐ   我爱你

lovely (*person*) kě ài   可爱

  (*thing*) hén hǎo   很好

low dī   低

luck yùnqi   运气

  good luck! zhù nǐ hǎo yùn!   祝你好运!

lunch wǔfàn   午饭

mail yóujiàn   邮件

mailbox (*at home*) xìnxiāng   信箱

make zuò   做

makeup huàzhuāngpǐn	化妆品
man nánrén	男人
manager jīnglǐ	经理
Mandarin Pǔtōnghuà	普通话
Mao Tse Tung jacket zhōngshānzhuāng	中山装
map dìtú	地图
market shìchǎng	市场
married: I'm married wǒ jiéhūnle	我结婚了
martial arts wǔshù	武术
matches huǒchái	火柴
material (cloth) bù	布
me wǒ	我
it's for me zhè shì géi wǒde	这是给我的
medicine yào	药
meeting huì	会
melon guā	瓜
men's restroom nán cèsuǒ	男厕所
meter mǐ	米
middle: in the middle zài zhōngjiān	在中间
midnight: at midnight bànyè	半夜
mile yīnglǐ	英里
milk niúnǎi	牛奶
mine: it's mine shì wǒde	是我的
mineral water kuàngquánshuǐ	矿泉水
mirror jìngzi	镜子
Miss xiáojiě	小姐
mistake cuòwù	错误

money qián	钱
Mongolia Ménggǔ	蒙古
Inner Mongolia Nèiměng	内蒙
Outer Mongolia Wàiměng	外蒙
month yuè	月
moon yuèliàng	月亮
more gèng duō	更多
more than bǐ . . . duō	比...多
morning zǎoshàng	早上
mosquito wénzi	蚊子
mosquito net wénzhàng	蚊帐
mother māma	妈妈
motorbike mótuōchē	摩托车
mountain shān	山
moustache xiǎohúzi	小胡子
mouth zuǐba	嘴巴
movie theater diànyǐngyuàn	电影院
Mr. . . . . . . xiānsheng	...先生
Mrs. . . . . . . fūren	...夫人
Ms. . . . . . . nǚshì	...女士
much duō	多
much better	好得多
hǎo de duō	
museum bówùguǎn	博物馆
mushrooms mógu	磨菇
music yīnyuè	音乐
must: I must wǒ bìxū	我必须
my . . . wǒde . . .	我的

narrow zhǎi 窄

near jìn 近

  is it near here? 离这里近吗?

  lí zhèlǐ jìn ma?

necessary bìyào 必要

necklace xiàngliàn 项链

need: I need a . . . wǒ xūyào . . . 我需要...

needle zhēn 针

Nepal Níbóěr 尼泊尔

nephew zhízi 侄子

never cónglái bù 从来不

new xīn 新

news xīnwén 新闻

newspaper bàozhǐ 报纸

New Year Xīnnián 新年

  Happy New Year! Xīnniánhǎo 新年好

New Zealand Xīn Xīlán 新西兰

next xià yíge 下一个

  next to . . . zài . . . pángbiān 在...旁边

nice (*person, weather*) hén hǎo 很好

  (*meal*) hǎochī 好吃

  (*town*) hén hǎo 很好

niece zhínǚ 侄女

night yè 夜

  for one night yīyè 一夜

no bù *see page 10* 不

  I've no money . . . 我没有钱

  wǒ méi yǒu qián

noisy hénchǎo 很吵

noon: at noon zhōngwǔ	中午
north běi	北
nose bízi	鼻子
not bù	不
not for me wǒ bú yào	我不要
nothing méi yǒu shénme	没有什么
now xiànzài	现在
number hàomǎ	号码
nurse hùshi	护士
occupied (*restroom*) yǒurén	有人
of . . . de	...的
the name of the hotel	旅馆的名字
lǘguǎnde míngzi	
office bàngōngshì	办公室
often jīngcháng	经常
oil (*motor*) yóu	油
(*vegetable*) càiyóu	菜油
OK hǎo	好
old (*person*) lǎo	老
(*things*) jiù	旧
on zài . . . shàngmian	在...上面
on the roof zài fángdǐng	在房顶
on the beach zài hǎitān	在海滩
one yī	一
that one nèi yíge	那一个
onion yángcōng	洋葱
only zhǐ yǒu	只有
open (*adj.*) kāile	开了

opera gējù	歌剧
Peking Opera jīngjù	京剧
opposite: opposite the . . .	在...对面
zài . . . duìmiàn	
optician yǎnjìngdiàn	眼镜店
or huòzhe	或者
orange (*fruit*) gānjú	柑桔
(*color*) júhuángsè	桔黄色
orange juice júzhī	桔汁
other: the other lìng yígè	另一个
our(s) wǒmende	我们的
out: she's out tā bú zài	她不在
outside wàimian	外面
over: over there zài nàlǐ	在那里
oyster háo	蚝
pack (*of cigarettes, etc.*) bāo	包
package bāoguǒ	包裹
paddy field dàotián	稻田
page yè	页
pagoda tǎ	塔
pair yìshuāng	一双
pajamas shuìyī	睡衣
panda xióngmāo	熊猫
pants cháng kù	长裤
paper zhǐ	纸
pardon? nǐ shuō shénme?	你说什么?
parents fùmǔ	父母
park (*noun*) gōngyuán	公园

(verb) tíngchē	停车
parking lot tíngchēchǎng	停车场
party *(celebration)* wǎnhuì	晚会
(group) tuántǐ	团体
pass *(mountain)* guānkǒu	关口
passport hùzhào	护照
path xiǎolù	小路
pavilion tíngzi	亭子
pay fùqián	付钱
can I pay, please?	我可以付钱吗?
wǒ kéyǐ fùqián ma?	
pen gāngbǐ	钢笔
pencil qiānbǐ	铅笔
penknife xiǎodāo	小刀
people rén	人
pepper *(spice)* hújiāo	胡椒
(red/green) shìzijiāo	柿子椒
per: . . . per cent bǎifēn zhī . . .	百分之...
per night měi yè	每夜
perfume xiāngshuǐ	香水
perhaps kěnéng	可能
perm diàntàng	电烫
person rén	人
pharmacy yàofáng	药房
photograph *(noun)* zhàopiàn	照片
photograph *(verb)* zhàoxiàng	照相
photographer shèyǐngshī	摄影师
phrase book duìhuà shǒucè	对话手册
pickpocket páshǒu	扒手

picture túpiàn 图片

piece piàn 片

  a piece of . . . yípiàn . . . 一片...

pillow zhěntóu 枕头

pin biézhēn 别针

pineapple bōluó 菠萝

pink fěnhóng 粉红

pipe (*smoking*) yāndǒu 烟斗

  (*water*) guǎnzi 管子

place dìfāng 地方

plane fēijī 飞机

plant zhíwù 植物

plastic bag sùliàodài 塑料袋

plate pánzi 盘子

play (*in theater*) huàjù 话剧

please: yes, please kéyǐ, qǐng 可以，请

  could you please . . .? 你能不能...?
  nǐ néng bù néng . . .?

plug (*electric*) chātóu 插头

pocket kǒudài 口袋

poisonous yǒudúde 有毒的

police jǐngchá 警察

policeman jǐngchá 警察

polite yóu lǐmào 有礼貌

politics zhèngzhì 政治

pool shuǐchí 水池

poor (*not rich*) qióng 穷

pop music liúxíng yīnyuè 流行音乐

pork zhūròu 猪肉

porter (*hotel*) ménfáng	门房
(*station, etc.*) bānyùn gōngrén	搬运工人
possible kěnéng	可能
postcard míngxìnpiàn	明信片
poster zhāotiē	招贴
post office yóujú	邮局
potato tǔdòu	土豆
potato chips zhá tǔdòupiàn	炸土豆片
pound (*money*) yīngbàng	英镑
prawn dàixiā	大虾
pregnant huáiyùn	怀孕
present (*gift*) lǐwù	礼物
pretty piàoliang	漂亮
price jiàgé	价格
problem wèntí	问题
pronounce fāyīn	发音
pull lā	拉
purse qiánbāo	钱包
push tuī	推
question wèntí	问题
quick kuài	快
quiet (*place, hotel, etc.*) ānjìng	安静
quite: quite a lot xiāng dāng duō	相当多
radiator sànrèqì	散热器
radio shōuyīnjī	收音机
railroad tiělù	铁路
rain yǔ	雨

it's raining xiàyǔ le	下雨了
rat láoshǔ	老鼠
razor tìdāo	剃刀
razor blades tìhú dāopiàn	剃胡刀片
read dú	读
ready zhǔnbèi hǎo	准备好
receipt shōujù	收据
record *(music)* chàngpiàn	唱片
red hóngsè	红色
refrigerator bīngxiāng	冰箱
religion zōngjiào	宗教
rent *(for room, etc.)* fángzū	房租
(verb) zū	租
for rent chūzū	出租
repair *(verb)* xiūlǐ	修理
reserve yùdìng	预订
restaurant fàndiàn	饭店
return *(come back)* fǎnhuí	返回
(give back) huán	还
rice *(cooked)* mǐfàn	米饭
(uncooked) mǐ	米
rice bowl fànwǎn	饭碗
rice field dàotián	稻田
rich *(person)* hén yǒuqián	很有钱
right *(not left)* yòu	右
(correct) duì	对
ring *(on finger)* jièzhǐ	戒指
river hé	河
road lù	路

roof fángdǐng   房顶

room *(hotel)* fángjiān   房间
  (space) kōngjiān   空间

rope shéngzi   绳子

round *(adj.)* yuánde   圆的

rubber *(material)* xiàngjiāo   橡胶

rubber band sōngjǐndài   松紧带

ruins fèixū   废墟

run pǎo   跑

Russia Éguó   俄国

sad shāngxīn   伤心

safe *(not in danger)* píng ān   平安
  (not dangerous) ānquán   安全

safety pin biézhēn   别针

salad sèlā   色拉

salt yán   盐

same yíyàng   一样
  the same again, please   再来一个
  zài lái yíge

sand shā   沙

sandals liángxié   凉鞋

sandwich sānmíngzhì   三明治

sanitary napkins wèishēngjīn   卫生巾

sauce jiàng   酱

sausage xiāngcháng   香肠

say: how do you say . . .   ...用汉语怎么说?
  in Chinese
  yòng Hànyǔ zěnme shuō . . .?

scallion xiǎocōng	小葱
school xuéxiào	学校
scissors jiǎndāo	剪刀
Scotland Sūgélán	苏格兰
screwdriver luósīdāo	螺丝刀
sea hǎi	海
seafood hǎiwèi	海味
seat zuòwèi	座位
seat belt ānquándài	安全带
second (*in series*) dì èr	第二
(*of time*) miǎo	秒
see kànjian	看见
I see! wǒ míngbai le!	我明白了！
sell mài	卖
separately (*pay*) fēn kāi fù	分开付
sesame oil máyóu	麻油
shade: in the shade	在荫凉处
zài yīnliáng chù	
shampoo xǐfàjīng	洗发精
shave guāhúzi	刮胡子
shaving cream guā hú pàomò	刮胡泡沫
she tā	她
sheet (*for bed*) chuángdān	床单
ship chuán	船
shirt chènshān	衬衫
shoelaces xiédài	鞋带
shoes xié	鞋
short (*person*) ǎi	矮
(*time*) duǎn	短

shorts duǎnkù	短裤
shoulder jiānbǎng	肩膀
shower (*in bathroom*) línyù	淋浴
shrimp xiā	虾
shut guān	关
shutter chuāngbǎn	窗板
Siberia Xībólìyà	西伯利亚
side street xiǎojiē	小街
sidewalk rénxíngdào	人行道
sight: the sights of . . . fēngjǐng . . .	风景...
silk sīchóu	丝绸
Silk Road sīchóu zhī lù	丝绸之路
silver yín	银
sing chànggē	唱歌
Singapore Xīnjiāpō	新加坡
single: I'm single wǒ shì dānshēn	我是单身
sister jiěmèi	姐妹
sit down zuòxià	坐下
skirt qúnzi	裙子
sky tiān kōng	天空
sleep shuìjiào	睡觉
slow(ly) màn	慢
small xiǎo	小
smell (*have bad smell*) nánwénde qìwèi	难闻的气味
smile (*verb*) xiào	笑
smoke (*noun*) yān	烟
do you smoke? nǐ xīyān ma?	你吸烟吗？
snake shé	蛇

so: so good zhēnhǎo   真好

  not so much búyào nàme duō   不要那么多

soap féizào   肥皂

soccer zúqiú   足球

socks wàzi   袜子

soft *(material, etc.)* ruǎn   软

soft drink ruán yīnliào   软饮料

sole *(of shoes)* xiédǐ   鞋底

somebody yǒurén   有人

something yǒuxiē dōngxī   有些东西

sometimes yǒu shí   有时

somewhere mǒuchù   某处

son érzi   儿子

song gē   歌

soon bù jiǔ   不久

sorry duìbuqǐ   对不起

  sorry? nǐ shuō shénme?   你说什么?

soup tāng   汤

south nán   南

souvenir jìniànpǐn   纪念品

soy sauce jiàngyóu   酱油

speak jiǎng   讲

spider zhīzhū   蜘蛛

spoon sháozi   勺子

spring *(season)* chūntiān   春天

stairs lóutī   楼梯

stamp *(for letter)* yóupiào   邮票

start *(noun)* kāishǐ   开始

station *(railroad)* huǒchē zhàn   火车站

steak niúpái	牛排
steal: my bag has been stolen wǒde bāo bèi tōule	我的包被偷了
sticky rice nuòmǐ	糯米
stockings chángtǒngwà	长筒袜
stomach wèi	胃
stop (bus stop) chēzhàn	车站
stop here tíng zhèlǐ	停这里
store shāngdiàn	商店
storm bàofēngyǔ	暴风雨
straight; it's straight ahead yìzhí cháoqián	一直朝前
street jiē	街
string xìshéng	细绳
student xuéshēng	学生
stupid yúchǔn	愚蠢
sugar táng	糖
suit (noun) xīzhuāng	西装
suitcase shǒutíxiāng	手提箱
sun tàiyáng	太阳
sunblock (cream) fángshàirǔ	防晒乳
sunburned shàihēide	晒黑的
sunglasses tàiyángjìng	太阳镜
sunshade yángsǎn	阳伞
sunstroke zhòngshǔ	中暑
suntan lotion fángshàijì	防晒剂
supermarket chāojí shìchǎng	超级市场
sure: I'm sure wǒ quèxìn	我确信
are you sure? nǐ néng kěndìng ma?	你能肯定吗?

surname xìng	姓
sweat *(noun)* hàn	汗
(verb) chūhàn	出汗
sweater tàoshān	套衫
sweet *(adj.)* tián	甜
sweet and sour tángcù	糖醋
sweltering: it's sweltering mēnrè	闷热
swim *(verb)* yóuyǒng	游泳
swimming pool yóuyǒngchí	游泳池
swimming trunks yóuyǒngkù	游泳裤

table zhuōzi	桌子
table tennis pīngpāngqiú	乒乓球
Taiwan Táiwān	台湾
take *(someone somewhere)* dàilǐng	带领
(something somewhere) dài	带
talk *(verb)* shuōhuà	说话
tall gāo	高
tampons miánsāi	棉塞
Taoism Dàojiào	道教
tap shuǐlóngtóu	水龙头
tape *(cassette)* cídài	磁带
(invisible adhesive) tòumíng jiāodài	透明胶带
taxi chūzūchē	出租车
tea chá	茶
telegram diànbào	电报
telephone diànhuà	电话
television diànshì	电视
temperature *(weather)* qìwēn	气温

temple miào	庙
tent zhàngpéng	帐篷
Terracotta Army Bīngmáyǒng	兵马俑
terrible zhēn zāogāo	真糟糕
Thailand Tàiguó	泰国
than bǐ . . . gèng	比...更
smaller than bǐ . . . xiǎo	比...小
thank you xièxie	谢谢
that: that woman nèige nǔrén	那个女人
that man nèige nánrén	那个男人
what's that nà shì shénme?	那是什么?
theater jùyuàn	剧院
their(s) tāmende	他们的
them tāmen	他们
then *(after that)* ránhòu	然后
(at that time) nà shí	那时
there nàlǐ	那里
there is/are yǒu . . .	有...
is/are there . . .? yǒu . . . ma?	有...吗?
there isn't/aren't . . . méi yǒu . . .	没有...
thermos bottle rèshuǐpíng	热水瓶
these zhèxiē	这些
they tāmen	他们
thick hòu	厚
thin *(thing)* báo	薄
(person) shòu	瘦
thing dōngxi	东西
think xiǎng	想
thirsty: I'm thirsty wǒ kóukě	我口渴

this: this street zhè tiáo jiē	这条街
this one zhège	这个
what's this? zhè shì shénme?	这是什么?
those nàxiē	那些
throat hóulóng	喉咙
through jīngguò	经过
thunderstorm léiyǔ	雷雨
Tibet Xīzàng	西藏
ticket piào	票
tie *(around neck)* lǐngdài	领带
tights liánkùwà	连裤袜
time shíjiān	时间
next time xià cì	下次
what time is it? jídiǎn le?	几点了?
timetable shíjiānbiǎo	时间表
tip *(money)* xiǎofèi	小费
tire *(on car)* lúntāi	轮胎
tired lèi	累
tissues báozhǐ	薄纸
to dào	到
to England qù Yīnggélán	去英格兰
toast *(bread)* kǎo miànbāopiàn	烤面包片
today jīntiān	今天
together yìqǐ	一起
toilet cèsuǒ	厕所
toilet paper shóuzhǐ	手纸
tomato xīhóngshì	西红柿
tomorrow míngtiān	明天
tonic *(water)* kuàngquánshuǐ	矿泉水

tonight jīntian wǎnshang | 今天晚上
too *(also)* yě | 也
  (excessively) tài | 太
tooth yá | 牙
toothbrush yáshuā | 牙刷
toothpaste yágāo | 牙膏
tour *(noun)* lǚxíng | 旅行
tourist lǚxíngzhě | 旅行者
tourist office lǚxíng shè | 旅行社
towel máojīn | 毛巾
town chéngzhèn | 城镇
traditional chuántǒng | 传统
traffic lights hónglǜ dēng | 红绿灯
train huǒchē | 火车
translate fānyì | 翻译
travel agent lǚxíngshè | 旅行社
traveler's check lǚxíng zhīpiào | 旅行支票
tree shù | 树
trip *(journey)* lǚxíng | 旅行
true zhēnde | 真的
trunk *(car)* xínglixiāng | 行李箱
try *(try out, test)* shì shi | 试试
T-shirt duǎnxiù yuánlǐng hànshān | 短袖圆领汗衫
tweezers nièzi | 镊子

umbrella yúsǎn | 雨伞
uncle shūshu | 叔叔
under zài . . . xiàmiàn | 在...下面
United States Měiguó | 美国

vacation jiàqī	假期
vaccination yùfángjiēzhòng	预防接种
vanilla xiāngcǎo	香草
vase huāpíng	花瓶
vegetables shūcài	蔬菜
vegetarian chīsù de	吃素的
very fēicháng	非常
Vietnam Yuènán	越南
village cūnzhuāng	村庄
visa qiānzhèng	签证
visit *(place)* cānguān	参观
(people) bàifǎng	拜访
voice shēngyīn	声音
voltage diànyā	电压
vomit *(verb)* ǒutù	呕吐
wait děng	等
waiter zhāodài	招待
waitress nǚzhāodài	女招待
Wales Wēi'ěrshì	威尔士
wall qiáng	墙
the Great Wall of China	长城
Chángchéng	
wallet qiánbāo	钱包
warm nuǎnhuo	暖和
wasp huángfēng	黄蜂
watch *(wrist)* shóubiǎo	手表
(verb) kàn	看
water shuǐ	水

141

we wǒmen	我们
weather tiānqì	天气
wedding hūnlǐ	婚礼
week xīngqī	星期
welcome: you're welcome bú kèqi	不客气
west xī	西
Western-style xīshì	西式
wet shī	湿
what? shénme?	什么?
wheel lúnzi	轮子
when? shénme shíhòu?	什么时候?
where? nálǐ?	哪里?
where is . . .? . . . zài nálǐ?	...在哪里?
which: which one? nǎ yíge?	哪一个?
whiskey wēishìjì	威士忌
white báisè	白色
who? shúi?	谁?
why? wèishenme?	为什么?
wide kuān	宽
wife qīzi	妻子
wind fēng	风
window chuāng	窗
wine jiǔ	酒
with hé . . . yìqǐ	和...一起
without méiyǒu	没有
woman fùnǚ	妇女
women's restroom nǚ cèsuǒ	女厕所
wood mùtou	木头
wool yángmáo	羊毛

word cí   词

work (*noun*) gōngzuò   工作

  (*verb*) gōngzuò   工作

  it's not working huàile   坏了

wrench huó bānshǒu   活扳手

write xiě   写

  could you write it down?   你能不能写一下?

  nǐ néng bù néng xiě yíxia?

wrong cuò   错

Yangtze Gorges Chángjiāng sānxiá   长江三峡

Yangtze River Chángjiāng   长江

year nián   年

yellow huángsè   黄色

Yellow River Huánghé   黄河

Yellow Sea Huánghǎi   黄海

yes shìde   是的

yesterday zuótiān   昨天

yet: not yet hái méine   还没呢

yogurt suānnǎi   酸奶

you nǐ   你

  (*plural*) nǐmen   你们

young niánqīng   年轻

your(s) nǐde   你的

  (*plural*) nǐmende   你们的

zipper lāliàn   拉链

zoo dòngwùyuán   动物园

Eyewitness Travel Guides titles include:

Amsterdam · Australia · Sydney · Budapest · California · Florida
Hawaii · New York · San Francisco & Northern California
France · Loire Valley · Paris · Provence · Great Britain
London · Ireland · Dublin · Greece: Athens & the Mainland
The Greek Islands · Istanbul · Italy · Florence & Tuscany
Naples · Rome · Sardinia · Venice & the Veneto · Moscow
St. Petersburg · Portugal · Lisbon · Prague · Spain · Madrid
Seville & Andalusia · Thailand · Vienna · Warsaw